M.

My First  in the

Classroom

50 Stories That Celebrate the Good, the Bad, and the Most Unforgettable Moments

Edited by Stephen D. Rogers

adamsmedia
AVON, MASSACHUSETTS

Published by
Adams Media, a division of F+W Media, Inc.
57 Littlefield Street, Avon, MA 02322. U.S.A.
www.adamsmedia.com

ISBN 13: 978-1-60550-654-8
ISBN 10: 1-60550-654-0

Printed in the United States of America.

J I H G F E D C B A

Library of Congress Cataloging-in-Publication Data
is available from the publisher.

This publication is designed to provide accurate and authoritative information with regard to the subject matter covered. It is sold with the understanding that the publisher is not engaged in rendering legal, accounting, or other professional advice. If legal advice or other expert assistance is required, the services of a competent professional person should be sought.

—From a *Declaration of Principles* jointly adopted by a Committee of the American Bar Association and a Committee of Publishers and Associations

Many of the designations used by manufacturers and sellers to distinguish their product are claimed as trademarks. Where those designations appear in this book and Adams Media was aware of a trademark claim, the designations have been printed with initial capital letters.

This book is available at quantity discounts for bulk purchases.
For information, please call 1-800-289-0963.

Acknowledgments

The editor would like to take a moment to thank some of his other teachers.

To Paula Munier (acquistions), Casey Ebert (copy chief), Matthew Glazer (project manager), and Denise Wallace (designer) of Adams Media fame, thanks for teaching me how a concept goes from pen to press.

To the members of my writing group, thanks for teaching me how to learn again.

To my wife and daughter, thanks for making every day a lesson in love.

Table of Contents

Contents

Introduction

MANY PEOPLE CLAIM their number one fear is public speaking.

Many of these same people are quick to quote George Bernard Shaw: "He who cannot, teaches."

Little do they know.

People who think the very idea of public speaking is scary should try teaching, which is public speaking to an audience that would rather chat amongst themselves, run around the classroom, or sleep with their heads on their desks.

To teach, one must do more than master the art of public speaking. One must also become adept at the arts of classroom management, social work, and juggling. Knowing the material to be taught is a definite plus, but sometimes a luxury.

When you step in front of a classroom, you're alone up there. From the moment your students waltz into the classroom until the moment they leave, you're on, and they're all looking at you to set the agenda, the mood, and the tone.

When you step in front of a classroom, you're joined by the memory of every teacher you ever had. Some provide examples for you to follow. Some provide mistakes for you to avoid. Some whisper in your ear, "You're losing them. Go back to the basics."

Your teachers taught you everything you know. Your students will teach you the rest.

Teaching—and especially teaching the first year—is not unlike riding a roller coaster, alternately thrilling and terrifying, filled with twists and turns, ups and downs—not to mention the occasional vomit.

Only those who can, teach.

And only those who can reflect upon their experiences in order to teach others the realities of a pedagogical career write stories such as the ones you're about to read.

This book is dedicated to all my teachers (in and out of the classroom), and the students who taught me so much more.

—Stephen D. Rogers

Preparing for a New Year

by Nancy Polny with Jessica Polny

IN LATE AUGUST, just before the rush of children, I began to prepare my first classroom for the upcoming year.

Imagining the room filled with all that childhood energy and noise, the quiet was a little unsettling as I organized the crayons and laminated the name tags. Perhaps the silence gave me too much time to think, because I slowly found myself becoming more and more nervous.

When I started working on my kindergarten classroom, I thought, "I can't wait to watch each little face learning and growing as the year passes."

As I stacked the glue sticks, I thought, "What if what I teach them doesn't stick?"

As I washed the math manipulatives, I thought, "What if my classroom becomes a hotbed of germs and I send my students home to infect their entire family?"

All my life I'd wanted to be a teacher, but now that the dream was coming true, I suddenly wasn't so sure I'd followed the right dream. Hadn't I also wanted to be a dancer at some point? Maybe that was the dream I should have pursued.

A deep breath brought me back to earth. Back to my classroom.

The last night before the first day of school, I didn't sleep a wink with the thoughts tumbling around in my head. Will my students like school? Will I be able to give them what they need? Will they make it through a whole day being away from Mom and Dad?

The first day of the school year dawned bright and early. Very bright. Very early.

Thanks to an excess of nervous energy and caffeinated tea, I was ready to face my students when the first bell rang and the buses whooshed open.

The children spilled out, chatting excitedly.

This, too, helped to make the moment more exciting for me, giving me another boost that helped me focus, kept me too busy to ponder second thoughts.

As my kindergarten students gathered in front of me, I saw that they were a little intimidated—not only was this their first day of school with a new teacher, it was their first day in the "Big School"— and I greeted them by the names I'd memorized when their parents had brought them to the open house.

"Sara, what a lovely backpack."

"Jason, how was your summer?"

As I spoke to them, each replied, a little timidly at first, but soon a grin would appear, spreading from cheek to cheek. I had noticed them. They were important to me. Everything was going to be okay.

"Robin, are those new shoelaces?"

Speaking to my students this way got them over their jitters, not to mention helping me to get over mine.

After settling into our room and listening to the morning announcements, the first task was to create a friendly environment and explain the classroom rules.

I smiled.

"My job is to keep you safe and happy. Your job is to be respectful and to learn. More important, your job is to have fun learning. I have lots of new and interesting things to show and teach you."

Their faces gazed at me with rapt attention.

I continued, "This might come as a surprise, but even I will learn new things, because you are never too old to learn. Are there any questions?"

Every child raised a hand. Some raised two.

"I'll answer all your questions, and I'll do it in the order you're sitting. Everybody gets a turn. Lakesha?"

And so it began as the children took turns talking. "Where do I go to the bathroom?" "When's our first fire drill?" "I forget."

In fact, most of my students "forgot" their question when I called on them, but at least they had fun raising their hands and being called.

"Do you have clay?" "Do you live here in this room?" "I forget my question."

As nervous as I was, they were more so, and it was my responsibility to help them get past those feelings.

I was doing more than teaching these students, I was laying the groundwork for their future education. I was showing them school could be fun, not something to be feared, or hated.

Calculus was not in my lesson plan. But someday, it would be in theirs, and what I taught them about learning would affect how they approached that course.

We read. We sang. We painted.

Preparing for a New Year

I gave out Band-Aids that made everything better and listened to jokes I heard over and over again.

We built. We created. We laughed.

All my preparation and hard work paid off. The day was filled with interesting tasks, with every minute scheduled to keep my students engaged.

The children were safe and happy. They were learning skills both practical and social.

Within minutes, it seemed, I watched them become confident learners as I taught them the classroom routines. The children beamed with pride at their independence.

As I took a moment to breathe, I observed how they interacted. Already they were treating each other like members of a team. Already, we had become an extension of their families.

By the end of the day, all memories of my earlier worry were long gone. The children had lifted me out of that negative space with their boundless energy and unbridled enthusiasm.

"Do we get to come back tomorrow?"

After my last student left, I straightened a few things and then just stood there for a moment in the middle of my classroom.

I loved this. I was a teacher.

Then I went home and took a nap.

Reluctant Journey

by Beth Schart

WHEN PEOPLE START their first job in an office, or a factory, or a field, they're starting at square one in the "job" portion of their life journey.

When you take a job as a teacher, square one was the first time you stepped into the classroom as a student. Your first year of teaching is hardly your first year in school. Remember the journey that brought you to the front of the classroom, and you'll know half of what you need to know to succeed.

I hated elementary school.

Many tearful mornings I tried with all my might to convince my mother I was much too ill to get out of bed, let alone go to school, but she just couldn't see it. (And she called herself a nurse.) Well, the years passed and I survived (as Mom had assured me I would). I don't remember exactly when, but as I got older I even learned to like school, and my memories of those mornings spent crying were nearly forgotten.

After college I took my place on the other side of the big desk, armed with all the important lessons I'd learned. I knew what to do if a child couldn't add and subtract. I had tricks up my sleeve for behavior management. I'd practiced teaching to a variety of learning styles.

When it was time to meet my students in the playground that first day, I felt prepared despite the butterflies in my stomach.

The schoolyard was filled with parents and children excitedly reconnecting with friends and classmates they might not have seen over the summer. Some kids actually shooed their parents away and reveled in the adventurous feeling of beginning a new year. As I took in this loud and mostly happy scene, my gaze immediately landed on one particular child who stood separate from the others. Plastered against her mother's side, the young girl attempted to lean and steer the woman back in the direction from which they had come.

Mom exerted gentle force in the direction of the other children, possibly hoping that a friend might spot her daughter and draw her in.

Their slight movement back and forth, almost a wavering motion, was not terribly obvious in all the bustle and activity, but it caught my eye.

I, too, was feeling a bit anxious about this new beginning. I was prepared, yes, but I remembered how I felt when I was in elementary school. I suddenly wanted my mother to step out of the crowd of mothers. "I'm here to pick up Beth. She needs to be home in bed. No need to worry, I'm a registered nurse."

This child and I seemed to have something in common. As I walked toward her with my disarming smile in place, I saw the tears.

"Hi. I'm a little nervous too. Probably because I'm new."

"I don't know why she's crying," her mother told me. "She seemed fine when we left the house."

"I think I understand." And to the child I said, "What grade are you in?"

I convinced her to take my hand and led her toward the third-grade line.

During that short walk, while it was just the two of us, I surprised the young student with the truth: "I never wanted to come to school when I was your age. I cried almost every day."

I didn't have to ask why she was crying. I already knew. And I hoped she knew I wasn't going to try to convince her that she was mistaken, that of course she enjoyed school. Who doesn't?

Lots of children don't.

Some children are shy, or socially immature, or just prefer a low-key environment. Some reluctant students are uncomfortable in the spotlight that we as teachers want to shine on everyone in order to draw attention to their achievements, great and small.

While most teachers realize the importance of subtlety when a child's actions need correction, subtle praise has its place as well. A wink, a shared smile, a gentle hand on the shoulder all communicate that the student is welcome and valued and well liked.

During eighteen years in the classroom, my bit of self-disclosure has served me on many occasions, putting both criers and non-criers at ease.

Maybe some of them will go on to become teachers.

Never Let Them See You Sweat

by Linda O'Connell

ALWAYS BE PREPARED! Never let them see you sweat! Those were just two of the tips drilled into me by my mentor, Helen Rogers, a veteran teacher with forty years of experience.

Mrs. Rogers told me that even though I was the mother of two young children, experience wiping snotty noses and messy bottoms was good but not enough. "When you're a preschool teacher, you need to be prepared for things that shouldn't be there, things that should, and things that weren't what they seem."

Not quite sure what my mentor meant, I focused on what I could control.

I set up my classroom to be visually stimulating, hanging everything at children's eye level. I readied all the materials. I organized the first day around music, movement, and rhythm, circle-time activities, and a selection of books certain to engage three- and four-year-olds.

Then Debi's mother arrived with a rat on her shoulder. A plump, beady-eyed, eight-inch-long rat. Eight inches excluding the tail.

My hands flew to my neck.

As I noticed Helen Rogers observing me, I remembered another pearl of wisdom: "Always offer choices."

Choices. I tried to calm my thumping heart while a prickly sensation told me I'd broken out in a sweat.

I bent down. "Debi, do you want your name tag up high or down low?"

By concentrating on my young student, I was able to put the rat out of my mind.

I then straightened to greet Debi's mother, trying my best to keep my eyes on her face, rather than the thing on her shoulder. "We'll see you at 11:30."

I smiled as I opened the classroom door, fully prepared to dart down the hall if the rat decided my classroom was too visually stimulating to leave.

"See you then."

I almost jumped when something landed on my shoulder. Even when I realized it was only the hand of Mrs. Rogers, my skin continued to crawl.

"You handled that very well." Mrs. Rogers nodded. "You passed your first lesson."

"Never let them see you sweat." Luckily, I'd dressed appropriately.

As I interacted with my students, my nerves slowly calmed. I could do this. My confidence continued to grow as the day smoothly developed according to my schedule, and nobody cried.

At circle time I asked probing, opened-ended questions. "Tell me about your favorite toy." "Tell me about your favorite television show." "Tell me about—" No, I wasn't going to ask about pets, just in case Debi's mother wasn't the only one with a rat.

The children jumped at the chance to share, all except Debi.

Out of the corner of my eye, I saw Mrs. Rogers making notes as I tried to coax Debi to talk. "Debi, I notice you're wearing pretty new shoes. Will you tell us about them?"

While I expected her to describe the cartoon character emblazoned on the side, Debi made a different choice. "My daddy's girlfriend bought them for me, but I can't tell my mommy that my daddy has a girlfriend," she lisped.

I immediately launched into an impromptu lesson on the famous cartoon character. Not only did I give myself time to regain my composure, I earned a nod from Mrs. Rogers.

My mentor's approval fed my growing sense of relief and pride.

As we approached dismissal, I passed out musical instruments, handing Debi the cymbals and encouraging her to bang them loudly. I'd teach that rat a thing or two about how loud and uninviting a classroom could be!

At 11:30 sharp, we marched out the door and into the hallway, where the parents waited, their faces beaming when they saw their children.

My eyes sought out Debi's mother. No rat. Where was the rat? I almost panicked, imagining the creature scampering up my leg.

I caught her eye and motioned at my shoulder.

She mouthed the words, "At home."

After my students and their parents were finally off, Mrs. Rogers congratulated me on my performance. "You handled those situations wonderfully. You have more patience than I do." She smiled and then continued, "You'll need it."

Right then, I thought she only added that last bit to throw some cold water on my ego, but Mrs. Rogers knew what she was talking about.

While Debi eventually overcame her shyness, Tommy resisted my attempts to draw him out.

Although I've successfully taught more than my share of special-needs children, some with severe medical conditions, Tommy was my first, proving that experience is key to being prepared.

Tommy wasn't even delayed; he was only hindered by a stuttering problem, but that was enough to confound me. No matter what I tried, I couldn't get him to respond verbally.

One morning, two months into the year, Tommy came into class so excited that he nearly threw off sparks.

Then he gave me a shock. He spoke.

"Miss Linda, I want to do show and tell today." He didn't stutter a bit.

I gathered the children immediately, and Tommy stood before the group to share.

"My mama's water pipe broke," he said.

"Where did it break?"

"In the kitchen," he said.

"What happened?" I couldn't believe how clearly and easily Tommy was speaking. While I would never wish a broken pipe on anybody, I had to admit that I was thrilled with the result.

My students leaned forward as Tommy continued telling his story. "Water got all over the kitchen floor and mama fell down and then Baby Gus slid right out of Mama's water pipe and I said, 'Mommy-Mommy-Mommy!' and she said, 'Tommy-Tommy-Tommy! Call 9-1-1.'"

Sometimes the surprises come so quickly that you don't even have time to sweat. That's when you'd best be prepared to laugh.

Never Let Them See You Sweat

My Open House Orientation

by Felice Prager

MISS HATHAWAY HAD been teaching at the high school where I landed my first teaching job longer than anyone else on the staff. Some of the other teachers actually had Miss Hathaway when they were students.

Everyone showed her the utmost respect.

Miss Hathaway taught American history, world history, and government. Eventually, every student at the high school would have to take at least one of her classes, and most grumbled.

I was told she wasn't mean or terribly difficult. The problem was in the presentation of the material. Miss Hathaway came from a generation of teachers who didn't believe in modifying her curriculum just to make it exciting.

I don't know how old she was, but to my twenty-two-year-old eyes, Miss Hathaway looked like a spinster.

She wore shades of gray and black. Her hair, another shade of gray, was worn in a forgettable manner. She was the venerable Miss Hathaway.

For the most part, I never saw her interact with anyone. Even in the faculty room, she didn't join and talk with the other teachers. She would eat a brown-bag lunch and grade papers.

Her very presence turned the mood somber. We teachers, who liked to kid around and relax on our breaks, acted as rigid and controlled as her students did when she was present.

At best, it was awkward.

During one of the early weeks of school, we had our open house, the evening when parents are invited to go through an abbreviated version of their child's schedule to meet the teachers and get an idea of what their child's day is like.

We teachers were told by our principal to present our curriculum and expectations in about five minutes. We were told not to get into specifics with parents about their children, but to follow the guidelines given.

The parents would then proceed to the next class, and in would troop a different group of parents.

I was nervous, to say the least.

While I did not mind being in front of teens, the thought of speaking in front of their parents unnerved me. I was afraid I would stutter and look inexperienced, especially since I'd been told to be serious and mature.

Even before the first day of school, I knew what I would be wearing for open house. I'd be dressed in my interview suit. I would wear heels. I would wear makeup.

I decided not to go home between the end of classes and 7 P.M., when the open house began. I carried an extra Diet Coke with me to tide me over, and a sleeve of saltines because I knew I would have a nervous stomach.

My Open House Orientation

Some of the teachers invited me to have an early dinner with them at a local diner, but I simply told them the truth, that I was too nervous to eat.

Instead, I sat in the faculty room, watching the clock and feeling my stomach grow tighter and tighter.

Then Miss Hathaway entered.

"Are you nervous?" she asked.

It was the first time I had actually heard her speak.

"Um. Yes," I replied. Then, "Very."

"Come with me," she said, as she held the door and indicated that I should follow her.

Her classroom was as orderly and gray as she was.

A "Welcome Parents" note waited on her blackboard with a neatly written "My Expectations of Your Child" written below in very precise cursive.

Miss Hathaway sat at her desk and indicated a seat right next to her, where I figured I was supposed to sit.

Then, with a smile, Miss Hathaway opened the bottom drawer of her desk and removed two coffee mugs and a bottle of Johnny Walker.

I was totally shocked, and I'm sure she saw it on my face. "Relax," she said as she poured some whiskey into each mug. She put the bottle back into the bottom drawer, lifted her mug, and said, "Cheers!" as she waited for me to clink my cup against hers.

"Cheers," I croaked.

"Don't worry," she added. "I have breath mints."

We didn't really talk.

Miss Hathaway sipped her whiskey in silence.

I drank and—with my empty stomach—giggled.

My First Year in the Classroom

"Oh, you're going to be fine," Miss Hathaway said.

She was right. But of course she would be right. She was the venerable Miss Hathaway.

When the other teachers got back from dinner, they found us sitting in the faculty room together, not talking, but smiling.

One of the teachers looked at Miss Hathaway and said, "I see you gave Felice her open house orientation, Mary."

I didn't know whether to blush or grin, and so I did a little of each.

Miss Hathaway simply nodded, and suddenly I knew that I wasn't the first to receive this gift from someone who knew how to approach open house.

Nor—I guessed—would I be the last.

Whupped

by Robin Amada Tzucker

THE SUPERINTENDENT GENTLY pointed out the possible negatives of the position: the school was in a rough part of town, the students were known as a tough group, and I didn't have any real experience working with poor and/or minority students.

Yes, I wanted to shout, and it's six weeks into the school year. I'll take the position. Yes!

Once I arrived at the school, the principal brought me into her office to make sure I understood the situation.

"I requested an extra teacher because I want to split up an extremely large class." She paused. "You should take two or three days and observe while you get your own room ready. That way you'll have a chance to get to know your future students."

"Sounds wonderful."

"Good. Why don't you get started then?"

Even better. I couldn't wait to meet the children and eagerly entered Mrs. X's room to begin my observation.

Chaos does not even begin to describe what I found in that classroom.

While Mrs. X stood up front lecturing, it was quite clear that not one of the thirty-seven fourth graders present was actually listening.

Several students chased each other around the back of the room. A group of five girls sat on their desks and painted each other's nails. A few students had their heads on their desks and were obviously asleep. The others chatted with their neighbors or soaked up the confusion.

As I stood there in horrified amazement, waiting for someone to notice I'd entered the room, I heard a loud THUD.

Mrs. X had thrown a blackboard eraser across the classroom at a group of students.

Nobody reacted. Not even the student who'd been hit.

To say I was in a state of shock would be an understatement.

I felt frozen in place, my stomach twisted in knots.

What would happen if I simply turned and ran, jumped into my car, and just took off? I could always go back to substitute teaching. Substitute teaching had been good to me while I'd waited for a full-time position to become open. Would it be so bad to go back?

I was spared finding out when a group of students nearest to the door finally spied me. "Yo, Mrs. X, there's a white lady here!"

Not exactly the welcome I'd been hoping for, but it would have to do.

Mrs. X walked over and introduced herself. She was an older African-American woman who was in her last year of teaching before she retired, and it was clear she'd pretty much given up.

"This is the laziest bunch of kids I've ever worked with. They don't know nothin' and they don't care. I don't know why I even bother trying to teach 'em anymore."

The students close enough to hear what we were saying watched us intently. We were possible entertainment. What was Mrs. X going to say next? What was I going to say?

I smiled at them.

They stared back with sullen faces and then averted their gazes.

Was it too late to turn down the position?

One day in that classroom was all I could take, and after school I asked the principal if I could start the next day with my kids. If the room wasn't quite ready, they could help me set it up.

The principal finally agreed to the plan, and I drove home wondering if I'd just made a terrible mistake.

That night I hardly slept, constantly waking from nightmares in which the students not only didn't listen to me, but actually overturned furniture, ran screaming from the room, and engaged in fights with one another.

I woke exhausted but excited, and more nervous than I'd ever been in my life.

At nine o'clock, I escorted eighteen of Mrs. X's students across the courtyard and into our new room.

The students flopped into their seats and stared at me.

I welcomed them to our new classroom, hearing the tremble in my own voice, feeling myself shake. "Do you have any questions?"

A girl raised her hand. "You ever teach kids like us before?"

"What do you mean?"

"I mean not white kids. There's no white kids here."

She was right, of course. I'd already learned there weren't any white kids in the whole school. A lot of African-American kids, a smaller percentage of Hispanic kids, and a smattering of kids from Southeast Asia. But none of the kids looked like me.

"I've been subbing in lots of schools around here, so yes, I've worked with lots of children who aren't white."

There was a silence.

Another voice spoke up, a boy in the back. Bobby. "You gonna whup us?"

"Umm . . . no. I don't believe in hitting kids."

"My momma whup me if I get in trouble at school. You gonna tell her if I get in trouble?"

My first day with my students, and already I'm facing a major ethical dilemma.

I held Bobby's gaze. Bright eyes flashed at me, a small grin on his face.

Taking a chance, I answered, "Maybe you'd better not get in trouble at school!"

The other kids laughed, and Bobby smiled at me. "Oooh, you gonna be a teacher," he said, drawing out the last word.

The class laughed again, and something inside of me melted.

Yes, these kids might be tough, streetwise, cocky. They might think they don't care, that they don't want or need to learn. It was my job to convince them otherwise.

My job. My classroom. My students.

I was whupped.

As I gazed at all their faces, I could feel myself feeling possessive. Yes, these were my students, and together we would build a community.

Together, we would learn.

High and Dry

by Sara F. Shacter

I HUNG THE maroon skirt and patterned blouse in my closet. Then I took them out again. Holding the outfit up to the light, I imagined walking through the school's main entrance.

Definitely not too casual. That's good. I don't want to look like a student.

I glanced back at the closet and spotted my gray suit. It was still a possibility. After all, a suit demands respect. Can't look unprofessional in a suit.

I hesitated.

No, a suit would be overreaching. It would scream "new teacher."

"Time for bed!" called my husband. "It's a school night!"

I smiled.

Confident I had chosen the perfect outfit—not too casual, not too pretentious—I hung the skirt and blouse so they wouldn't wrinkle. After all, I had to look my best.

Then I packed my bag: books, lesson planner, several pens (just in case the first seven or eight ran out of ink), a file of semi-frightening official forms, and a legal pad. Because the next day was teacher orientation, and not the first day of school, I wasn't sure I'd need all I'd packed, but better safe than sorry.

"You better be in bed, young lady!" I heard my husband chuckle.

I placed my bag by the front door. There. I'm wildly prepared, I thought. Clothes are picked and bag is packed. My anxiety eased, and I headed for bed.

The next morning, I woke before the alarm rang. My heart quickened. This was it! Teacher orientation. I would meet the other new hires and make my first impression on the administration.

In the bathroom, I turned on the shower. The water burst out of the showerhead. Then tapered off. Then stopped.

I fiddled with the faucet and tried again. Nothing.

No, no, no, I thought. A thread of panic unraveled in my stomach.

I yelled, "Joe, the shower's not working!"

My husband came in and fiddled. "I'll try the other bathroom."

I sat, nervous energy bouncing my legs up and down. This was not happening. Not to me, not today. A minute or two passed.

"Nothing!" he called.

My stomach lurched.

"Hey!" Joe stuck his head in the bathroom. "The clocks are out."

Adrenaline shot through my body. I ran past my husband into the bedroom and snatched my watch off of the dresser. Its face smiled up at me: six-ten. At least I hadn't overslept.

But there was no power.

Which meant no lights.

High and Dry

And no pumps to push water up to our apartment.

In other words . . . no shower.

I rushed to the mirror. My reflection and I yelped at one another. Bed head! I would greet the first teaching colleagues of my life with bed head!

And perhaps an odor.

My panic began to spiral.

Joe helped me to breathe.

Okay, I reasoned. I'll just start at the end of my morning routine. Maybe by the time I get to the shower, the power will be back.

I ate breakfast. The milk-softened cereal tasted like paste. The orange juice was not what my roiling stomach needed.

I laid my perfect maroon skirt and patterned blouse on the bed. I chose jewelry, shoes, and hose.

I brushed my teeth without using any water.

Counted to ten, slowly, for good luck.

Then I tried the shower again.

Nothing.

I had no choice. It was time to go.

I ran a comb through my bed head, slathered antiperspirant under my arms, and headed for the stairs.

Fifteen flights in ninety-degree heat. By the time I reached the bottom, a fine layer of sweaty ooze coated my body.

I flung myself into the car and slammed the door shut. A quick look into the mirror made me cringe. Now I had bed head *and* humidity hair. I didn't even want to risk a sniff under my arms.

I drove slowly, trying to give the air conditioning time to fix the damage. When I reached school, I summoned up every shred of self-respect I could muster and walked through the front doors.

After wandering the hallways, I found the meeting room, full of new staff and a few administrators I recognized.

I waved a general hello and chose a seat, careful to maintain a "smell free zone" around me. The meeting began. At least I knew all eyes were on the principal.

And thank goodness for the box of coffee just steps away. The rich aroma was probably filling everybody's noses.

Then came a break. The other new teachers began to form groups and chat.

I am going to die, I thought. Taking small steps to keep odor from drifting too far from my body, I kept my underarms clamped tight.

One of the new teachers caught my eye.

"Hi," he said.

"Hi," I cleverly replied.

"Boy, they're giving us a lot of information, aren't they?"

Information? "Yeah. It's been quite a morning!"

And then it all came tumbling out, the saga of the power outage.

While I poured out my story, people clustered around, listening.

When I finished, the sympathy began to flow.

"Oh, that's terrible!" said one woman.

"At least it didn't get you down."

"Well, tomorrow has to be better!"

We all laughed and commiserated.

Despite everything, relief washed over me, and I felt clean for the first time all day. My colleagues were lovely, and I had officially begun my dream career. Afterward, I drove home smiling.

Two days later, I would meet my first students. Sure, I was nervous. Sure, my lesson plans might tank.

But at least I wouldn't literally stink.

High and Dry

Coping

by Jacqueline Seewald

If you can look into the seeds of time,
And say which grain will grow, and which will not,
Speak then to me.

—William Shakespeare, *Macbeth*

I don't adjust well to change. Even though I'd been contracted to teach full-time in the very same high school where I had done my student teaching, I would be stepping into a classroom without the safety net of my mentor. I was mighty nervous.

My freshman classes were fine. I'd been advised not to smile at my students until at least after Christmas, and I took that advice to heart. I dressed professionally—investing in a number of conservative dresses and suits—and carried myself the same way. My hair was cut in a no-nonsense, short style, and I wore minimal makeup. I walked into the classroom carrying a leather briefcase that exuded a self-confidence I didn't particularly feel.

As I said, my freshman classes were fine.

However, everything fell apart the last class of the day. As soon as I entered the classroom of juniors that first day, there were whistles, hoots, and shouts.

"Hey," a particularly rough-looking youth called out, "are you really gonna be our teacher?"

I suddenly realized these "boys" were not much younger than I was, a fact that hadn't really struck me when I was warned that the class consisted mostly of students who would not be going on to college, many of them with learning disabilities, and a few who had already been held back.

They were obviously impatient to leave for the day, and at that moment, so was I.

While I placed my briefcase on my desk, I tried to set the necessary tone, and failed.

They were a rowdy, disrespectful group. Even worse, while I didn't have enough experience yet to manage them, Butch did. Butch was an expert at stirring up trouble.

Recognizing I would have a difficult time maintaining discipline while Butch was determined to do the opposite, I tried to engage him in the lessons.

When I called on him to read aloud, however, he became hostile and flatly refused. Only later did I discover he could barely read.

I adjusted my plan once again, each change raising my discomfort level.

Rather than ask the students to read, I did. I also read the assignments aloud, and talked about the authors we were discussing in order to get the students interested.

When I later learned the students didn't take books home—or even bring them to class—I created my own library in my classroom, distributing textbooks and study guides every day, holding each student's bus pass until the materials were returned.

I also was responsible for providing pens and pencils.

But I was reaching my students. Despite their problems and negative attitude, I was getting them to learn.

Whenever Butch cut, the rest of us actually discussed what we were reading. The students thought about their responses and expressed them. They paid attention.

When he was present, Butch created one disruption after another. He was a clever instigator who always managed to not to overstep the boundaries. He had no intention of learning and was intent on making certain others didn't learn either.

One afternoon, he arrived late for class, saw the other students were listening intently, and proceeded to smash a chair violently into another student.

This time he'd gone too far. I was sick of letting Butch run my classroom. I needed to get him and his disruptive behavior out.

Butch's guidance counselor frowned. "The thing with that boy is he has a really bad home life. His father's an abusive alcoholic. The boy's angry at the world in general."

"I'm sympathetic," I said. "But I can't have him back in my classroom. He's depriving everyone else of an education."

"I'll see what I can do."

Butch was reassigned to a class with a much more experienced teacher.

For once, I welcomed change.

As for the rest of the class, things immediately improved. Students who had been resistant or grudging moved closer to acceptance.

And then we hit Shakespeare.

The curriculum called for me to teach *Macbeth*. I'd always loved Shakespeare and knew the play forward and backward. But how did I interest students who could barely read contemporary English?

I put the traditional teaching plans aside.

"I'm going to read from the play and maybe you can help me by taking some of the parts. I know the words will sound kind of odd, but remember this was written a long time ago. It sounds funny to everybody."

Seeing that they were still with me, I continued, "We'll talk about each part. You can stop me to ask questions so that we all understand what we're reading."

Remembering my first day in this classroom, it was a little hard to believe that we were actually tackling Shakespeare, but tackle him we did.

I acted out the scenes as I read the play, my students joining me in bit parts.

When we weren't reading, we discussed the play in detail. The blood. The gore. The psychology.

The students loved Macbeth the soldier. I couldn't help wondering how Butch would have responded to the conflicted troublemaker. Perhaps a more experienced teacher could have used the play to help Butch gain a better appreciation of his situation.

One of the most valuable lessons I learned that first year was confidence, confidence that I could cope, that I could be flexible and adaptive. The classroom is a dynamic place, each student totally unique, and sometimes contradictory.

The basic tenets of teaching might be set in stone, but everything else changes.

Even me.

The Beginning
of Hope

by Dr. Sharon A. Lynch

Land of Hope and Glory, Mother of the Free
How may we extol thee, who are born of thee¿
> —Arthur Christopher Benson, British poet

As the notes of the processional to graduation rang in my ears, I scanned the bright, hopeful faces.

You would never guess from the shining confidence of these students the contents of their medical records, the breadth of diagnosis found there: cerebral palsy, rubella syndrome, deaf-blind, severely mentally retarded, nonverbal. Yet here these students stood, or sat in wheelchairs, graduating from their training program, feeling good about who they were, and ready to face whatever joys or sorrows that life had to offer.

Could young people with such limitations offer anything to a world as tangled as our complex society¿ Of course they could. They could offer simple things such as love and joy, faith and understanding.

My thoughts traveled back to my first day at the Center nine years ago. As a substitute teacher, I approached the early childhood room to which I had been assigned with apprehension and fear. Did I have the inner strength to do this?

Honestly, I didn't know.

Opening the door, I saw a little three-year-old strapped onto some sort of stretcher frame. I greeted her, patted her arm, and talked to her a bit. The only response that I got, however, was a roll of her eyes, drooling, and a moan.

"I wonder if they are all like this," I thought to myself. "Maybe she's in better shape than most."

The teaching assistant approached me. "Her name is Tina. Feel what that babysitter did to this poor child," she said, pointing to the back of Tina's head.

As my hand stroked her beautiful hair, my fingers told me they were touching a washboard rather than the head of a child. "Dear God," I thought, "How can you allow such a thing to happen?"

I continued talking to Tina, telling her who I was, and that I had come to help.

She responded to my voice, but I don't know if the words meant anything to her.

During the day I was busy helping the children climb stairs, mold play dough, and play musical instruments. I helped Tina do as much as she was able, in addition to comforting and feeding her.

The assistant informed me that Tina rarely slept during naptime and it was my duty to keep her quiet.

The Beginning of Hope

As I rocked Tina, I felt the stiffness of her limbs relax, and then I heard her laughter. Behind the drooling, the twisted arms, and the smell of a body that she could not control, Tina was a joyful soul who responded well to love and attention.

My heart went out to her.

Alone in this room filled with children with disabilities, I thought, "Dear God, I do not know who you are or what you want of me. But I do know this: If these children are to be my life and my work I will need your help. I just can't do this on my own."

There is something very humbling and unsettling about these children. They hold the power to change the lives of others if we are willing to accept that change.

Throughout the year I became acquainted with many more of our children at the Center. After I was able to break through their initial reluctance and hesitation, nearly all of these children showed themselves to be joyful, determined students who took pride in their small accomplishments.

When I was offered a contract in the unit for older children with severe disabilities, I was ecstatic. Even though it would mean additional schooling, I greeted this new experience with a sense of excitement.

During my years in the classroom, I learned something new every day and went to bed tired every night. I received the most precious gift any teacher, poet, or statesman could ever hope for—the unconditional love of my students.

Regardless of the external circumstances, Lloyd was always ready to pat my back and hug my neck when he sensed that I felt sadness. No matter how overwhelming the classroom might seem, Alex was always ready to sympathize with his expressive eyes, since he had no voice.

As is written in 1 Corinthians 13, "Love is not rude, it is not self-seeking, it is not easily angered, it keeps no record of wrongs . . . Love never fails."

I was blessed in receiving this unconditional love, given through the hearts and hands of these children. It took only one year of receiving this unconditional love through the arms and faces of these children for me to acknowledge the God who created them.

When others question the validity of the life of a child with disabilities, I know they are both shortsighted and blind to the truth. I had spent many days and nights searching, but never came close to knowing who God is—or His great love for me—through those efforts.

Instead, it has been through His children that I have come to know these things, and I thank them for that gift from the bottom of my heart.

Cerebral palsy, rubella syndrome, deaf-blind, severely mentally retarded, nonverbal—they are placeholders on a yardstick that measures us all. Everyone falls somewhere on the continuum. You. Me. The children with whom I work.

These children have every reason to anticipate life's joys and sorrows, to embrace whatever challenges or blessings come their way.

What more could anyone hope for?

Rumors

by Kari-Lynn Winters

MORE EXCITED THAN a kindergartner on ice cream day, I couldn't sleep a wink the night before the first day of school.

I'd picked the perfect outfit for the perfect day. And my first day teaching would be a perfect day.

My classroom was ready. My knapsack was packed. My lunch was in the fridge. Even the car was gassed.

Seven sleepless hours later, I drove to the school, my heart nearly pounding out of my chest. While I drove, questions swirled through my mind. Would the kids like me? Would they listen to me? What would the staff and the parents think of me?

As I pulled into the parking lot, I waved to the staff members I had met during preparation week. There was Mrs. Bemberton, the principal, with shoulder-length blonde hair and a crooked smile. Mr. Wilson, the physical education teacher, was looking buff and tanned. And there was Ms. Ferris, supposedly the strictest teacher in the school.

Rumor had it that if you chewed gum in her class, you'd have to go to her swap jar, put your wad of gum in, and take someone else's out. Apparently, she'd watch to make sure you chewed the piece you took.

I think it was safe to say that Ms. Ferris didn't have many problems with gum chewing in her classroom.

When the children began to arrive, I greeted them at the door. How could these innocent-looking children be labeled behavioral?

I tried to assure each of the parents that his or her child was in good hands and that I was well qualified to be teaching. However, one parent, who had a particularly innocent-looking child, glanced at me as though I'd come from another planet.

"Excuse me," she said bluntly, "but if my son is too much for you, and I am sure he will be, just send him over to Ms. Ferris. She has permission to whup him."

My mouth dropped. "Whup him?"

The mother nodded, her coarse black ringlets falling into her eyes. "That's right. Teach him some manners, if you know what I mean."

"Ah . . . um . . . I don't think . . . um . . . that will be necessary."

She rolled her eyes, roared with laughter, and then turned to leave. "Trust me," she said blankly. "You don't know my son. Adea is a handful."

His mother talked about her son's behavior as if she'd had no part in his upbringing. Yep, he's a handful. No idea how that happened. No idea at all.

My morning only got worse. Of course there was the regular behavioral issue of defiance, children refusing to do their schoolwork. And there was the usual calling out and chasing one another around the desks. And then there was the not uncommon issue of students throwing papers, erasers, and even chairs. But it was the student choking to death that really caught my attention.

I'd asked my first graders to graph colors and had given each child a set of small, colored candies. I told them not to chew these sweets.

Felicia, who loved to dance, stood up and started to boogie because of course that's the proper way to usher in a new math lesson. I asked her to sit down, and she did.

A minute later, however, she was up again, dancing.

"Sit down," I repeated.

She refused to listen. It was then that I noticed that her brown skin was turning gray. And then it dawned on me: she's choking!

I started to panic, using language inappropriate for the classroom. Finally, I shouted, "Call Mrs. Bemberton! Somebody help me!"

When no one came, I started the Heimlich. I balled my fist, wrapped my hands around Felicia's small waist, and began to thrust upwardly into her abdomen. I was surprised at how much force was necessary for this maneuver to work, since Felicia was literally picked up off her feet.

The other students watched in horror. "Ms. Winters," they called. "Whatcha doin'?"

"Quiet please," I cried out. "I need to concentrate."

Adea explained to the other students, "This is what Ms. Winters does to you if yer bad!"

Then, as if magic, two things happened. First, every kid in the class sat down quietly. And second, the bright yellow candy shot out of Felicia's mouth with such force it nearly knocked over a chair.

Exhausted, we both collapsed. Felicia groaned. A while later, I called her mom and asked that Felicia be picked up. When her mom arrived, she was hollering. Not only was she extremely worried about her daughter, she was also upset that she had to leave work early on the first day of her new job.

I thought, you can count yourself lucky!

From then on, I was rumored to be the new strictest teacher on the planet, as the gossip quickly spread. The tale stated that if you were bad in my class, I would cuss at you, pick you up under your arms, lift you off your feet, and break each of your ribs one by one.

And then, if that wasn't bad enough, I would make you suffer for a while (from your broken ribs) before sending you home to get in even more trouble from your mama.

After that first day, I barely had any trouble in my behavioral class.

Other teachers commented on the great success I'd had with my students. Mr. Wilson said he couldn't believe what I'd accomplished. "Those kids are like angels."

Even Adea's mom was later forced to admit to me, "My son never had such a successful year."

It's truly amazing how powerful (and beneficial) rumors can be!

You just might want to think about starting one.

Student Teaching

by Kimberlee Rizzitano

THERE I WAS, FORTY-SOMETHING, a former help desk manager for a *Fortune* 500 company, and someone who quit corporate life to be with her young children. While at home, I decided it was fun to be with children. I liked teaching them things. So, of course, I could go back to school and get a master's degree in elementary education. And I did. As a part of this program, I was required to do fifteen weeks of student teaching. I could do that. Right?

So there I stood, an official career changer, mother of two, and . . . a student teacher. I was standing in a classroom of twenty-three fourth graders, and all that was going through my head was, "What was I thinking?"

The students were all eyeing me as if wondering what I was doing there. I was looking at them thinking that they all looked so sweet and innocent, but I knew that could not be. The teacher I was working with had given me a very brief overview of the class, the schedule of their day, and what I was expected to do. I thought, I can do this.

The first few weeks, I did great. I kept reminding myself that I was doing fine. It was okay. I can do this. This is not bad. It is fun!

When I was about nine weeks into the student teaching thing, the teacher decided I should take over a literature circle. We went to the library and picked out the book *Bunnicula*, by James Howe. This is a great story, but it has really advanced vocabulary for the fourth graders in my literature circle. So I took the book home, read it, laughed at many parts of it, and created a workbook. This way the students could go chapter by chapter and understand what we read and keep track of the vocabulary words that were tricky. The teacher liked my workbook, and I was all set to begin my own serious literature circle.

I showed my students the book and workbook and explained my plan. We previewed the book, made predictions, and settled down to read the story. I guess I should tell you that literature circles in this classroom are a very serious thing. You cannot bother the teacher when she is directing a literature circle. She is responsible for listening to the oral reading or directing the students on what they need to do. As I sat down to begin my literature circle, however, I noticed that the rest of the students in the class kept looking over at us. I was not sure if it was envy or pity that was on their faces.

See, by nine weeks into my student teaching, every student in the classroom knew I was not the serious type. Oh, I am all for learning, and everything has its place, but they knew if you can have fun along the way, I would find it.

As you may have guessed, I was a bit nervous as my literature group started to "popcorn read" the book. Each student took a page.

I helped them with the tough words, and we wrote down vocabulary words they didn't understand. Then they looked at me. I thought, "What?" They said I should take a page and read it too, so they could hear how it "should" be read. So I did.

Now, if you have ever read *Bunnicula*, you may understand what happened to me next. I was reading the part where Howard the Dog eats a green sour ball. The author of the book, James Howe, goes into a lot of detail on how poor Howard reacted to it. I started to laugh uncontrollably. Soon, tears were flowing down my face, and I had to take my glasses off to wipe my eyes.

The literature circle students were all jumping up to get Kleenex.

I could not stop laughing. The entire classroom was now looking at me and they could not help but laugh at me!

Finally the "real" teacher came over and said, "What are you doing?"

I was just getting back in control. I said, "This part of the book is so funny. I can just picture the dog doing these things. I'm so sorry—I'm back in control now."

I stood up and faced the class of fourth graders, who were still looking at me and the literature circle with total envy because we were having such a great time, and said, "I'm sorry I bothered you. This book is very funny at times. We won't disturb you again."

Later that morning during snack time, one little girl came up to me and said, "Mrs. Rizzitano, it's okay that you got silly. I love when you do things like this. I used to complain to my mom that I didn't like school, but since you have come, I love it. Really, I come to school every day just so I can see what you will do next. Can I be in your literature circle too?"

That's when I realized maybe I did make a good career-change choice.

I was doing something right. This little girl hated to read, but she was willing to participate if I made it fun. Although I have not used *Bunnicula* again, I do try to make students realize that school is what you make it.

If you think it's a drag, it will be. If you think it is exciting, it may be. And if you have me for a teacher, you never know what I may do next. One thing is for sure; it will be within the curriculum frameworks, and I expect a lot from my students, but we do have fun along the way.

Not to Mention the Python

by Judy Nickles

THIS NEW TEACHER was two weeks late for her first day of school, not an auspicious beginning.

Because my visa was delayed, I missed the opening of classes at the American School of Kinshasa in the Democratic Republic of the Zaire (formerly the Belgian Congo), scarcely six years after the country's difficult independence from Belgium and only some eighteen months after the bloody Simba Rebellion.

With only a weekend to look at my books and prepare, I faced my class on Monday morning with trepidation. Here were fourteen boys and girls culled from the other sixth grade, taught by a more capable, experienced teacher.

Why had these children been chosen? Why had the other teacher let them go? I tried not to think the worst. Perhaps I was being given the students who wouldn't be held back by the fumbling efforts of a first-year teacher.

My students were mostly missionary children who lived in hostels because their parents worked far away on isolated stations. Some were children of the American military, which was in Zaire in an advisory capacity. Others had parents with businesses in the city.

The United Nations had nothing on my classroom.

Wearing the casual clothing that I would soon adopt, my students welcomed the new teacher—if not their new classroom—with smiles.

As the latecomer, I was assigned the only available classroom in the sprawling white stucco building. Its windows were grated but glassless. The noise of nearby construction made it impossible for us to hear each other—or even to think!

We moved to the upper half of the auditorium, from which we were booted regularly whenever the high school drama department needed to rehearse. Those days meant a patient packing of books and supplies before trudging uncomplainingly—well, almost—to the basketball court or, on rainy days, to the small library.

We had desks and an easel blackboard, which doubled as the scoreboard for Friday night basketball games. On Monday mornings, I dispatched two or three boys to retrieve it, although rain over the weekend would put the board temporarily out of service.

While the children could only display their work on the folding door separating the two halves of the auditorium, they did so with tape and pride. They then put it up again when the humidity loosened the tape, or the door was thrown open on performance nights.

The children were not only quick learners, but also hardy and generous.

What's the standard gift for teacher? An apple? Not for me that year. Instead, almost every morning I found on my desk a piece of rather dry cinnamon toast, an offering from the children who lived in the nearby hostel.

One morning, instead of the toast, I found the tail of a freshly killed python, which I was told had just breakfasted on someone's animal. Witnessing the snake's execution by machete, one of my students begged the tail for me.

Recognizing the honor it represented, I said all the right things, and then relegated the python tail to the bottom drawer of my desk.

Maybe a piece of dry toast wasn't that bad after all.

I only taught in the mornings, since older students used the building in the afternoons. A new, larger school was being built, farther away than the construction that drove us from that first classroom. Despite the shortened day, I, like probably every new teacher before me, ran out of lesson plans before running out of time.

Similarly, the students, like probably all students everywhere, represented a broad spectrum of academic challenges. I felt woefully inadequate to meet them. Whatever the learning styles and needs of each student, they had only one very new, very green teacher.

I taught them what I could as best I could. Somehow, they learned.

I was a naive twenty-one. If I was homesick at my age, what was it like for them at eleven and twelve to be away from their parents for such long periods of time? If I was disturbed by reading about the violence visited on the missionary community, what was it like for them to have lived in this environment?

Watching them accept their situations with grace and good humor, how could I complain about mine?

When washing and grooming wasn't possible because of the erratic availability of electricity and running water, my students didn't stop learning. I couldn't stop teaching.

How earnestly they regaled me. How fervently they explained, demonstrated, and advised! In essence, they became my teachers.

Outside the classroom, I rarely refused an invitation to join their games of foursquare, something akin to, but more challenging than, hopscotch.

I watched my students make their own entertainment during unstructured recesses. A ball, a jump rope, a piece of chalk, and their own boundless enthusiasm made up for whatever recreational equipment and facilities they might lack.

They supervised themselves at play, made their own rules and enforced them. They were kind to each other. I don't remember ever having to intervene.

Today, forty-odd years later, I don't need the yearbook picture to remember their faces and their names. Other students from other classes have faded from memory, but not these children. They were special. They were my first. They were mine in a way that no others could ever be.

Today, they would be in their fifties. They are parents, perhaps even grandparents. Where are they? What have their lives been like?

Whatever I gave them, they gave me so much more.

Not to mention the python tail.

That Which Does Not Destroy Me

by Melinda Huynh

The secret of teaching is to appear to have known all your life what you just learned this morning.

—Author Unknown

It was my first day as a substitute teacher. It was a day I'll remember forever.

Trying to overcome my anxiety about being in a classroom alone for the first time with more than twenty students, I thought to myself, "Just be calm. You'll be fine. Breathe."

It was a fifth- and sixth-grade combo class, which I later heard is one of the most difficult class structures to manage. Of course, being new and fresh into the teaching field, I walked through the door with a positive outlook and motivated mindset. I thought, "If I change the life of one person in this class, I am doing the world a great justice. It's going to be great!"

Boy, was I proven wrong.

The majority of students had major behavior problems, some of which I had encountered before in my observations, but others were at the more extreme level. The students did not have a regular teacher at the time, and had gone through six different substitutes the previous week, none of whom would come back for a second day.

A selected group of students had been in and out of the office due to day suspensions. The staff and principal resorted to day suspensions because they had run out of ideas, and thus the students almost enjoyed being suspended because it meant they didn't have to learn or do any work.

This was the class who provided me my introduction to teaching.

It was in this class that a student stood up in the middle of our math lesson, yelled curse words at the top of his voice, and then shouted how much he hated school and learning.

Even though I was appalled and frustrated, I tried to keep my composure.

I sent the student to the principal, saying in a firm yet secretly trembling voice, "If you don't want to learn, you don't belong in my class. Some of us are here to learn."

Even though I didn't yet have the personal resources to do anything more for this student, I felt like the cruelest person in the world.

My job was to teach, not to punish. Yet if I didn't discipline, nobody was going to learn.

Later, as I was writing on the board with my back turned to the class, someone threw an eraser at my head. No one was responsible, and so I declared they were all responsible. "Everybody in this room just lost recess today."

Little did I know that taking recess away from hyperactive kids who needed physical activity to burn off excess energy was punishment all right, but the teacher was the one who paid the price. Me!

You might think that after reaching such a low point, things could only get better. Ha! This class was out to destroy me.

That day, I wrote detentions for three students, suspended six, and expelled one.

My first day on the job.

The first day of my longed-for career.

Did I quit? No. In fact, I returned to that very classroom the next day.

"Ms. Huynh, you came back! No one has ever come back to our class because we are so bad."

I paused, allowing a little smirk to show on my face. All I could think of saying at that moment was, "Well, today is a new day, isn't it?"

The students had expected the detentions, suspensions, and expulsions. What they didn't expect was a teacher who seemed determined to teach them, no matter how difficult and disruptive they tried to be.

They had tested my boundaries. Oh, how they had tested my boundaries.

They had assumed that I—like everybody else—would quit on them in frustration.

Well I showed them.

And they showed me . . . a surprising amount of respect, so much so that it still bewilders me. That second day went very smoothly, nothing at all like my first day in that class.

Yes, some of the more troubling students were absent. But it was more than that.

My determination to teach them showed a commitment to them, indicated that they were worth teaching.

If I was willing to respect them as people, they were willing to respect me as a person and teacher.

Would I always be able to show such calm composure when faced with an unruly classroom? No. Nobody is perfect. Not even a teacher!

Teaching requires patience, compassion, and flexibility. The reality of the field is that it forces teachers to be multifaceted individuals: caring yet firm; nurturing yet not too nurturing; outgoing and innovative, yet able to stay within the standards.

We do better some days than others. We're human, after all.

Each and every day is a new learning experience. If one day you work on managing your classroom effectively, the next week you will work on smoother transitions, and the next month you will work on discipline and rewards, and so on, and so forth.

The next year you might even have to scratch everything you mastered and try new procedures and systems for a new group of students. It's all a matter of trial and error, and that's the beauty of it!

When I think back to my first day teaching, I have to laugh—enough time has passed.

I will never forget the students of Room 28. They may have tried to destroy me, but I would not be who I am today if it were not for them.

That which does not destroy me, makes me stronger.

—Friedrich Nietzsche

Coming Full Circle

by Sharon Blumberg

IN LATE AUGUST of 1992, I was hired to teach Spanish at a junior high school in Illinois after staying home for eight years to raise my own children. If I could successfully parent, I could certainly teach.

¡Dios mio!

While I'd filled in for some long-term subbing assignments, that wasn't the same as running my own class for an entire school year. By October, I realized I needed outside help managing both classroom behavior and course material.

The veteran teacher next door offered me advice on teaching self-control. "Whenever they start to talk amongst themselves, just turn off the lights. They'll get it eventually."

Well, the students didn't. As soon as the lights came on again, they resumed talking.

And so I tried to teach above the din until, frustrated, I'll flick the light switches again.

I finally realized how futile my efforts were when one of my students yelled, "Ooooh noooo, not the lights!"

I was in the dark, the students were in the dark, and nobody at all was learning.

So much for going to another teacher for help. Next, I turned to the principal.

The principal, who was in his late forties with graying hair, had managed this school for twenty years. While he was nearing the end of his career as principal, and would soon move on to higher duties within the district, he spent many, many hours with me after school.

Like any good student, I diligently worked on my daily lesson plans and classroom management strategies with his guidance. Even to this day, I don't know if he ever realized how much he helped and influenced me.

While I finally had a modicum of control in the classroom, I still wasn't lighting any fires behind the eyes of my students.

Once again, I looked outside. As January rolled around, I knew I needed to do something to combat a dark and cold midyear slump. Suddenly, an idea came to me.

"How about writing to the authors of your textbook? Let's find out what kind of work goes into putting together a textbook program."

The students responded with enthusiasm. "How do we do that?" "Will they answer?" "What should we ask?"

"First, we need to work on putting together your questions. Raise your hand if there's something you'd like to ask, and I'll write it down."

Together, we put together a letter, which I showed to my class before mailing:

Dear Señora Valette,

I am a seventh- and eighth-grade Spanish teacher at X School in Illinois. My Spanish classes are studying under your program and my students and I have some questions to ask you. If you would be kind enough to answer them at your earliest convenience, I would love to post the answers to this letter in a framed plaque to put on display for my classes. These are our questions:

- How old are you?
- Do you have any children?
- What is your native language?
- How many languages do you know, and how did you learn Spanish?
- How long did it take you to coordinate the whole *Spanish for Mastery* program?
- Could you tell us anything about the illustrator of this program?
- Will you be publishing any upcoming books or programs?
- What inspired you to coordinate this program?
- Are the advice columns real in the textbook?
- Can we have an autographed photo of yourself?
- What type of work do you do at the university?

Sincerely,
The Spanish students of Señora Blumberg

I wasn't sure exactly why this group project invigorated the students, but it did, and the class returned to their regular studies with *mucho gusto*.

Even better, I was finally able to prove that their hard work had paid off when we received a letter from Señora Valette.

My students were tickled and proud when I shared her response, along with her autographed picture.

Her answers were quite thorough with one exception. When it came to her age, Señora Valette wrote, "If you really want to find out my age, you can look it up in Who's Who in America."

While I hunted down a suitable frame for her letter, my students surprised me by investigating further, reporting to me several days later that they'd learned her age because they followed her advice and looked it up in the library.

They'd set out to learn something? On their own?

Some of my students further astounded me by saying they wanted to become Spanish teachers and write their own textbook some day. These were the same students whom I had once needed to quiet by turning off the lights.

As a veteran teacher, I still use some of the same strategies that I developed that first year, and promote their use to the teachers I mentor. A key component of those strategies are four basic rules that are set in stone:

- Come to class prepared
- Be respectful to everyone
- Raise your hand to participate
- Be ready for instruction by the bell

My first year, I may not have come to class prepared or been ready to instruct by the bell, but I certainly am now. Experience has taught me. After looking ever outward, I looked inside at what I'd learned to become the teacher I am.

Coming Full Circle

With the Accent on Foreign

by Susan Peters

New York City in 1969 was a tough place to get a teaching job for a Midwesterner still figuring out the bureaucracy of certification. I'd thought a Phi Beta Kappa (with honors in English) and a master's degree in German would have principals begging to hire me. Instead, I was stuck doing temporary office jobs until mid-October, when a call came from the local high school.

The foreign language teacher had received his draft notice, and the principal asked, "Could you start next week?"

"That would be fine." I hung up the phone, jumped up and down, and grabbed my husband to celebrate.

When I showed up on Monday, however, I discovered that in addition to first- and second-year German, I would also be teaching two first-year Spanish classes.

"Actually," I told the principal as he was filling out the Temporary Emergency Substitute form, "I don't know Spanish."

I'd hesitated before admitting this fact, mindful of my husband's modest salary, our ever-shrinking bank account, and the depressing prospect of an endless stretch of filing, typing, and taking dictation. The only Spanish word I knew was *Adios*, and I didn't want to hear it.

The principal nodded toward the pile of texts. *"Buenos días. Gracias.* Just stay a lesson or two ahead of the students. You'll do fine."

There were two things I had heard about teaching foreign language in high school: a) You get the brighter, college-bound students; b) Unlike English or math, which is old and boring by now, foreign language is a novelty, often taught by actual foreigners with French or German accents.

At my high school, Madame Maheu and Herr Schneider commanded respect; they knew a secret code, having lived where people used these odd-sounding words to communicate.

I'd spent several summers in Germany communicating with actual Germans, and prided myself on having a near-native accent. When I finished my first class of the day—second-year German—I felt pretty confident.

Then the first of my students for the two Spanish classes filed in. I smiled encouragingly, waited until they settled in their seats, and introduced myself. I told them I'd be taking over for their other teacher, and that I was looking forward to getting to know them.

And then I took roll, using the seating chart.

The seating chart consisted of twenty-five small cards, arranged in five rows of five cards each, set in a heavy cardboard folder. When the cards were properly inserted into their slots, only the first name of each student was visible; this saved teachers time because they could scan the room, turn over the cards for the missing students, and enter the absences later.

Since I wanted to learn everyone's full name, I pulled each card out and read both first and last names.

Slowly, an ominous fact dawned on me: at least a third of the students had Spanish surnames. As I plowed through Gomez and Menendez and Ortiz, I began to wonder why these kids were taking a first-year class.

There were two possible explanations: a) Their parents had been so eager to assimilate that no Spanish was spoken at home, and these students wanted to connect to their culture through the language; b) The students already spoke Spanish and they took the course looking for an easy grade.

If the latter explanation was the correct one, I was in big trouble.

Putting all those Spanish-sounding names aside, I asked the class to review the previous lesson. I had them do that by taking turns reading the dialogues aloud, and then closing their books and giving me the Spanish vocabulary when I said the English word.

The only Spanish I spoke that day was a cheery *Adios!* as they left.

By the time my husband got home that night, I'd formulated a plan. He'd had two years of Spanish in college; he would help me with the pronunciation of new words, and as far as the grammar went, I'd take the principal's advice and keep a couple of days ahead of the students.

Things seemed to go well for a while. Third-period Spanish always went smoothly, probably because I'd had the previous hour to practice, but it was the first Spanish class of the day that became increasingly worrisome.

The problem was the carryover from first-period German, where I would remind students that *stecken* and *sprechen* were pronounced "shtecken" and "shprechen," and then an hour later I'd hear myself saying "Hashta la vishta," as if I were coming off a three-day drunk binge in Tijuana.

Finally, Gloria Ortiz spoke up. "That's not the way Mr. Belfer pronounced it."

I thought fast and addressed the class. "You know, there are many different kinds of accents in Spanish. There's Castilian, where the 's' is pronounced 'th,' and Catalan, and of course there is a slight difference in each of the South American countries. Ecuadorian Spanish, for example, does not sound like Peruvian Spanish."

My husband grinned when I told him what I'd told my students. "Yeah, you have a different kind of Spanish accent—from the extreme northeast. Like around Munich."

The next day, I went to the principal and told him I was sorry, but I just couldn't continue faking the Spanish, and would have to stop teaching those two courses at the end of the semester—several weeks away.

A few days later, the principal told me another teacher was willing to take them. "You'll just swap your Spanish courses for his English ones."

Gracias.

And thus that spring I found myself teaching another foreign language: Shakespeare.

Preconceptions

by Barri L. Bumgarner

"MAN, I HATE to read. Why do I hafta take this class?" Shoes kicked at debris littering the deck outside my classroom. Slow, trudging feet clomped toward the door as I stood silently nearby. Some of them probably mistook me for a new student.

"Yeah, reading sucks."

Slight murmuring at the sight of couches and chairs. No desks. Only one round table in the back. Bookcases lined the walls. More low rumbling. This was sorta cool, the vibe said, but no one was willing to admit it—they had preconceptions.

Preconceptions. These students didn't know me, as this was my first year. They didn't know what was going to happen in my class, as it hadn't started yet. And they were already grumbling.

More students clamored toward class. The comments pelted the outside of the trailer like a spring hailstorm. "Ugh, reading . . ." A few wandered into the trailer, silent, looks of wonder on their faces, but for the most part, their expressions were filled with dread.

It's okay. I waited. I let them watch me smile, wondering who I was.

Is that the teacher?

I expected their negative comments. In their minds, to see "Reading" on their schedule meant they were lacking the skill. In truth, their skill level had absolutely nothing to do with why most were enrolled, which had to do with the management of teacher-student ratios.

The mystique of my classroom gave me an edge. They stepped off the security of their wide-legged preconceptions, and now they were off balance.

I knew something they didn't, that they would be quick to shout down as ridiculous: they loved to read. Every single one of them. I was going to prove it.

None of these kids truly meant it when they said they hated to read. What they meant was that they hated being made to read. Or they hated reading what they were assigned in school. Or they just hated to be told to do anything.

Nothing thwarted a student's love of a good book more than being forced to read it by Monday at 8:00 A.M. To discuss it in front of their peers. And then to be tested on the content. Or expected to write a paper.

On a high school exit survey, most students admitted they once liked to read. The number one reason for it turning into dislike? A teacher.

One of my own teachers told me that. This dared me to think outside the box of educational preconceptions.

The comments faded as the students sat, anticipating what they were sure would be another boring, assignment-filled class. But the atmosphere had them slightly unsure. The comfortable seats, sports posters, inspirational signs, and my barrage of Kansas City Chiefs and St. Louis Cardinals memorabilia already told them a bit about me, but not enough to give them an edge.

The stuffed bears spread throughout the room had to spike their interest a bit, too.

When everyone had found a spot, I started, almost like it was a conversation and class hadn't really started yet. "Who in here has a MySpace page?"

Hands shot into the air.

"Facebook?"

More hands.

"So do you spend a lot of time chatting with friends, blogging? What do you like best about going to those places?"

Comments formed a steady hum of energy.

Finally, one kid mumbled that he stayed up well past midnight chatting with friends, well after his parents thought he had gone to bed.

"So what do you all do while you're on MySpace or Facebook?"

A few mischievous grins.

I had enough new-teacher confidence to believe I could handle the situation, whatever they said. Most of the students blurted, "Read blogs, write messages, listen to music . . ."

It was my turn to grin. "So you read a lot."

There was a sudden blanket of silence, and then nods. Eyebrows rose. Someone said, "Well, it's different . . ."

I pulled out a book and told them, "I'm going to be talking about five or six books a day for the first two weeks or so. Kind of like a movie trailer for a book, and this first one . . . *TTYL* . . . any of you heard of it?" I didn't give them time to answer. "It's about some students who text and instant message each other. The whole book, that's all it is."

I leaned forward, as if sharing a secret. "And get this, there's a sequel called *CUL8R*. More texts and IMs. Totally cool, and they gab about teachers who're driving them crazy, friends who are talking about them behind their backs. They're all just starting high school and sort of fall into different cliques. Any of you think about those kind of things?"

Whatever their preconceptions, the students were with me, their posture having changed while I talked. They stared at the book like they were going to dive for it.

I immediately launched into some of my A-list books. *A Child Called "It." Forged by Fire*. I followed those with an excerpt from *The Pact*, and the opening staggered them.

Keeping the momentum going, I finished with books including *Among the Hidden*, *Stuck in Neutral*, and *Shattering Glass*.

"So, how many of you would like to read stuff like this?"

Hands shot into the air. Some kids mumbled that they never knew about books like these. Others were still subdued, but the hunger was in their eyes as they stared at the books sitting on the edge of my desk.

As the kids left that first day, the attitudes were different, and the rumblings not even remotely similar to those heard fifty minutes earlier.

"Man, this class is gonna be cool . . ."

"Yeah, we read what we want."

"I'm glad I got Reading."

"Me, too. Which one are you gonna read first?"

The comments continued until they faded around the corner. I smiled.

My students weren't quite putty, but they definitely had started to move in that direction.

Two Years for the Pain of One

by Beth Morrissey

MY FIRST YEAR as a teacher was spent in the library, and my first year as a librarian was spent in the classroom. Unfortunately, they were the same year.

When I was hired to be the librarian of a private international school, I was fresh out of graduate school. I was young and dynamic, not to mention well-schooled in information literacy instruction. What more could I need to implement a research skills program across the entire secondary division?

Quite a lot, as it turned out.

The secondary school was composed of years 1–6, or the equivalent of both middle and high school. Recent changes to the curriculum meant that for the first time, students would not be assessed strictly by one final exam. Instead, they would have to submit coursework, which would be reviewed by both their teachers and external examiners.

Although I was a first-year teacher, the veteran teachers were not in any position to advise me in this case. They didn't know what to make of the new curriculum either.

Due to unforeseen circumstances, I couldn't even enter the library until the first day of school. The band's instruments were cluttering my office, books returned at the end of last year were sitting in piles rather than on the shelves, and the tables were arranged in a rather odd blockade.

Eventually, the space was arranged, and I was ready to welcome my classes.

What I hadn't counted on was every single class from every single year, one after the other after the other. It seemed like every teacher in the school viewed me as a babysitter, and couldn't wait for my classes so that they could have a coffee break.

I was shocked. I was hurt. And then I was delighted.

Left to my own devices, I went on to meet every student in the school. We traveled on information treasure hunts together. We made bibliographies of our favorite graphic novels. We held heated discussions on using wiki sources in scholarly research. We also dug into the causes of World War II, the formulation of bubblegum, and the size of worldwide sport fan bases.

Little by little, the other teachers joined in the fun, except for a few who still viewed research as a waste of time.

By Christmas, I understood the teachers' objections. They were concerned only with knowledge, something they felt would best accumulate by lectures and only lectures. But both the new national Irish curriculum and I were concerned about the students learning how to learn.

As the majority of teachers came to realize the importance of research skills, they came to see the link between research and knowledge. For possibly the first time in their lives, they saw the beauty in devising questions and answering them, synthesizing facts into well-informed opinions, and developing thesis statements based on the evidence that they had collected.

No longer were these teachers concerned whether their assigned projects and papers were "too American" or "not educational enough."

They embraced the new curriculum and opened themselves to the experience of learning again.

Unfortunately, not all the teachers had this epiphany.

"The Hold-Outs," as I privately nicknamed them, made everyone's year a nightmare. Every project deadline was met with their grumbling. Every time one of their students asked them about research, the Hold-Outs responded with shrieks of indignation. A student even came in to tell me that she had been berated for outlining an essay exam before writing it.

For months I tried to squash my bitterness toward these teachers. By the time the first spring flowers were budding, I wondered if I'd get an ulcer from swallowing my displeasure.

Then, one warm afternoon, I was sitting in the library with a geography class. I had students on the Internet researching countries, and students in the stacks tracing maps.

The library door was open and we all could hear the shouts of the primary school students next door. What we didn't hear was the library door shut quietly as one of the chief Hold-Outs wandered in.

When I finally noticed her, she was firmly installed at a back table. For the entire period, she worked alone in that corner, but I noticed her looking up every now and then if the students called answers to each other or otherwise made a peep.

That whole class, I cringed, certain she would reprimand me at the end. The bell rang and she came over to me.

I almost bit through my lip as I prepared for a heated showdown.

"Beth," she said, laying a hand on my arm, "I didn't understand. I thought the kids liked doing 'research' because it got them out of class. I didn't see that they were still doing work here, just a different kind of work."

My eyes filled with tears as I told her how much her words meant to me.

She handed me a hanky and smiled.

"If I had known this earlier, I would have brought my classes down here a lot more," she confessed. "I'll have to do that in the future. But I won't be back to do my grading. Too many kids doing too much learning in here for that."

I couldn't have been happier.

By the end of my first school year, I was no longer concerned with the Hold-Outs.

Instead, I was busily coordinating the schedule for the next year: my second year as teacher-librarian.

It's All Good

by Dr. Andrea S. Foster

"CAN YOU START tomorrow?" Mrs. Manna, the principal of St. Joseph Parochial school, said looking very tired.

Tomorrow.

I'd only graduated two days before with a BS in curriculum and instruction, receiving my Texas Life Certificate for teaching kindergarten through eighth grade with a specialization in art.

While my plan had been to work on my master's degree in education, an admired professor suggested that gaining teaching experience simultaneously while completing my graduate program might be a wise move.

"I'd love to," I said.

After I signed my first-year contract for a seemingly relieved Mrs. Manna, I was officially a sixth-grade teacher.

Mrs. Manna took me on a tour of the school building and introduced me to my future classroom. Even though I could see that the building was old and in need of great repair,

I still only barely contained my shock when Mrs. Manna opened the creaky classroom door.

The room was large with windows on both sides. Between lay trash, debris, and at least a summer's worth of dirt and dust. The classroom smelled of must and mold. And it was hot . . . really hot!

"There's no air conditioning, but plans for ceiling fans are in the works," Mrs. Manna assured me.

I was speechless.

Mrs. Manna looked at me apologetically and promised she would get the custodians to open the windows and air out the room if I wanted to stay and decorate my classroom with bulletin boards.

Bulletin boards? I was going to need buckets of Lysol and some serious scrub brushes first.

I spent the next eight hours cleaning out my classroom. I called in for some reinforcements in the form of my boyfriend, who owned a store downtown. When he arrived at St. Joseph's and observed my classroom space as well as the copious amount of sweat dripping down from my face, he said with great emphasis, "Quit! Quit now!"

Well, I did not quit. Nor did he remain my boyfriend for long.

After I spent the day clearing the classroom of debris and scrubbing the walls, I put up a few inspirational posters. I also unearthed a dilapidated blue wooden teacher's desk (As a student would one day remark, "That teacher's desk is pathetic!").

I placed my grade book, a fresh desk pad, and pencil holder on my desk. I knew then that I was ready for my students. I had no curriculum guides, no technology, no framework for teaching kids of this age. I was operating on pure adrenaline.

Little did I realize the challenge this first class would offer. Not only did I have the principal's son, as well as the Texas A&M University president's son, I had the most heterogeneous and wildly eccentric group of twelve-year-olds that one could imagine.

I had one student who was gifted with a photographic memory and could spell any word in the English language. I had another who punched the brick wall every time he received a low grade on an assignment, when he bothered to turn one in.

The class was self-contained, which meant I taught all subjects: mathematics, language arts, science, social studies, art, music, reading, and religion. Furthermore, each grade level took turns being responsible for planning the weekly masses and the hymns.

I created my own curriculum and activities, relying heavily on the units and lesson plans I had developed in my teacher preparation classes at the university. Most of my lessons were derived based on need and creativity.

For example, since the windows remained open most of the day for air circulation, my students had trouble keeping their papers on their desks. This led me to organize frequent geologic expeditions to the field just past the playground to collect rocks.

We observed and measured our rocks before classifying them as igneous, sedimentary, or metamorphic. We wrote stories about our rocks. Then we painted them (rock art!) while listening to classical rock music. After the activities, each student named his or her favorite pet rock and then used the rock as a paperweight.

As the year progressed, I worked hard to get to know each of my students personally. By the spring, I had met with all the parents on several occasions. Going above and beyond the call of duty, I even helped the president of Texas A&M and his wife by helping transport their son from home to school when they were on vacation.

Invariably, the sixth grader would hide from me to make us both late for school. Determined not to be, I enlisted the help of the household staff, who would alert me to his whereabouts. He never figured out how I knew where he was hiding, and one day I overheard him tell a classmate, "Miss O really does have an extra set of eyes. I swear she can see through walls!"

Miss Ognibene, my Sicilian maiden name, was difficult for my students to pronounce that first year, which is why we shortened it to Miss O.

On the last day of school, one of my students surprised me by announcing to the class that he had looked up the meaning of my maiden name. "*Ogni* means 'all' and *bene* means 'good.' 'Ognibene' means 'all good.' "

I was touched when everybody clapped.

Almost thirty years have passed since then, but I can still recall each one of those nineteen students. I remember their names, their academic achievements, and how we grew as a community in the classroom by developing an amazing sense of respect for one another.

Little did I know that teaching those nineteen students would teach me much more than I could ever learn in any textbook or methodology course. Little did I appreciate at the time the curriculum lessons I learned from just opening some windows for the air.

Learn about your students and make the classroom come alive.

It's all good!

Mrs. Psycho Loses Her Place in English Class

by Beverly C. Lucey

WHEN I GOT MY first teaching job, I was assigned to a team for eleventh-grade English. Three of us, in ten-week cycles, would teach all the juniors.

I was the radical who was going to try everything I could to make high school better for my students than it was for me.

Mrs. B was a very dignified, middle-aged woman who had gone to Radcliffe, married well, lived well, taught well, and tried very hard to maintain standards.

The third member of our team was Mrs. S, who had a Polish last name that sounded enough like Syko-something that students called her Mrs. Psycho when she wasn't within hearing. She was menopausal, a vague area of murky new emotional territory that can turn a teacher weird, if she weren't a bit of a character already.

Mrs. S was a squat fireplug of a woman. She also was a smoker, a drinker, and a serious card player who lived in a room in town during the week, far away from her no-good gambling husband. She was also a very smart and very sensitive poet.

Mrs. B and Mrs. S were my mentors. They made up the schedules, divvied up the work, and made encouraging noises.

Mrs. B helped me find books, get settled, and fill out forms. More important, she provided emergency cookies.

Mrs. S was a dispenser of succinct advice. In her gruff whiskey voice she said: "Listen, Honey. Don't ever teach the verbs to lay and to lie. And don't teach the poem, 'There is no frigate like a book.' Anything they can turn into something dirty they will. Watch out or you'll step in it. That's all you have to know and you'll do fine."

School began. It was exciting, exhausting, scary. But I had my mentors.

Mrs. S was all glower and "I mean business" from day one. At four-foot-seven, she could make a linebacker whimper with a look from her baleful eye. Mrs. S was a rock. If she heard the slightest cuss word, the offender would be banished. A hint of an obscene gesture would get her temper up. "An outrage, these students. No respect. Driving me to drink."

By a very cold November, she started having hot flashes and insisted that all the windows remain open. Any student who complained was sent to the office for insubordination. Mrs. S—Mrs. Psycho—only seemed to get worse.

Her voice came clearly through the wall separating our rooms. "Ken! Sit up straight. Angela! Does your mother know what you are wearing? Jonathan? Did I just hear you say something rancid? I know the priest at your church. Do not get on my last nerve, Raymond. Do you hear me? I said, Do. You. Hear. Me. This is my classroom, and in my classroom we behave like ladies and gentleman. Pretend if you have to, but that's the way it is. You will learn a civilized tongue. And let me tell you, you are very lucky that, in this state, we can no longer hit students. Hah."

One lovely spring day Mrs. S appeared especially frazzled. The class periods were shortened due to an upcoming assembly, and she snapped at every random stretch or ambient sound.

"Mark! Jeremy! Collect the books. We're done with *Ethan Frome*. Sit back down, I haven't marked down the numbers yet. No. Stand up. Collect them and let Melinda cross off the numbers. Now! Take them into the English closet and bring back the set of books I left on the counter there. What are you waiting for?"

Since my students were happily working away on their journals—probably pretending not to listen to the goings-on next door—I decided to step out into the hall and observe.

Chaos. The students were up and down and crashing into each other.

I was about to enter the room when Mrs. S regained control.

After glaring her students into submission, she told them how important English was, how language mattered, and how they would learn to appreciate the power of words whether they wanted to or not. She ranted about their future and bemoaned their never reading anything decent on their own. She told them they'd never get into college if they didn't start taking more care with their work. They needed to sit up straight and speak carefully. They needed to say what they meant. And think before they spoke.

She paused and made a sweeping glance around the room as if daring anyone to defy her.

Mrs. Psycho Loses Her Place in English Class

A peacemaker—I knew the type—raised his hand and pretended enthusiasm. "Mrs. S? What do we get to read next?"

I could feel the wave of relief pass through the students. Mrs. S was obviously pleased by the question. Disaster had been averted.

"Class, we will now begin one of the greatest books in American literature. One I know you will love for the classic that it is. Class? I know you will be challenged by this great book from the American canon."

Long, dramatic pause. Another grand sweep of the room. Mrs. Psycho, who never let a mistake go unnoticed, made a Spoonerism out of "Huckleberry Finn."

A Sharp Memory

by Billie Wilson

WHENEVER I WAS ASKED what I wanted to be when I grew up, I'd say, "A teacher."

A teacher scribbled with snowy chalk on a shiny blackboard. She sat at an impressive desk decorated with an apple from an adoring student. She supervised others performing tasks that she assigned.

I wanted to purse my lips and look down my nose like my teachers did, and say, "Certainly, Philip. You may be excused. Number one, or two?"

Growing up with pious parents just before and during World War II, every Sunday I ensconced myself into a polished mahogany pew at Bug Swamp Baptist Church, the religious and cultural center of my youth.

Ladies in our church possessed at least one trait in common. No civilized woman past puberty pulled on a dress until she'd struggled into a girdle.

I marveled that Sister Sadie McBride could somehow manage to bend her knees and plop into the Amen Corner pew without bursting right through the seams of her sausage wrappings. Clarissa Wright's armored, bean-pole body had it no easier. Whether stick-thin or rain-barrel-rotund, females attending our church crammed their unyielding forms into garments suitable for torture.

Some girdles contained vertical strips of whale bone sewn into unforgiving fabric, rendering free movement next to impossible. Dear Grandma Nettie laced up her 111 pounds every Sunday morning into just such a thingamabob.

In the spring of 1954, after sixteen years of schooling, I closed my English books and claimed my diploma. Summer sped past, and my first day as a teacher at North Myrtle Beach High School dawned.

Attempting to squelch nervous jitters, I told myself, "I can do this. I'm all grown up." After all, wasn't the inner-tube-like contraption I wore the epitome of adulthood?

I remember powdering its insides, stepping into the girdle, then tugging, yanking, until, finally, the aggravating retainer settled into place, rendering all softness impenetrable, or almost so.

Principal Brown kept all new teachers in his office, explaining procedures, until the bell for first period sounded. By the time I approached my room and opened its door, thirty-two pairs of young eyes pinned me to the blackboard. Carefully I placed my books onto an apple-less desk. A thought entered my head: if I were five years younger, these kids would be my peers! I desired nothing more than to bolt for the door.

I'm a teacher, I reminded myself.

Steeling myself for a long day in the company of what appeared a group who would most likely prefer playing in the nearby pearly strand, I smoothed my pleated, pink plaid skirt before sitting at my desk. Time for roll call.

"Bob Anderson!"

"Here," a hoarse voice erupted from a wee lad, his nose supporting spectacles that dwarfed his face.

"Addie Bass!"

"Present!" Addie, an older-looking brunette, sighed as if she'd prefer being anyplace else.

"Betty Cox."

A diminutive blonde sang out, "Here!"

At that point I distinctly felt something pierce my derriere. The jab wasn't painful, just sharp, like a slight pinprick. I settled into my chair. The prick became more pronounced.

"Leonard Dawsey."

"Here, teacher." This tanned, shaggy-haired young man grinned from ear to ear. "You feel good today, teacher?"

"Fine, Leonard. Thank you."

"Hazel Gore."

"Here."

What a pretty girl! Dark, curly hair, with hazel eyes, just like her name!

"Teacher!"

"Yes, Leonard!"

"You sure you feel okay?" Not waiting for an answer, the young man rose, paper in hand. "I got a poem to read."

How strange. "Later, Leonard."

After all enrolled students had answered as present, I instructed them to take out paper and pencil, planning to have them write a short autobiography.

A Sharp Memory

Leonard Dawsey stuck up a finger. "Now?"

I shoved back my chair. Pain jabbed my bottom. "Okay, Leonard." I frowned, seeking a different sitting angle. "Read your poem."

"Leonard writes one for every occasion," Lily Sellers volunteered. Leonard grinned, shuffled from one foot to another, and read:

There once was a teacher brand new.
She may have bit off more than she can chew.
She came to the beach
Said here she would teach.
She didn't know our school was a zoo.

"Thank you, Leonard. You've written a limerick. A five-line poem."

"It's got five more lines." When Leonard continued to read from what looked like a bare page, I realized he was composing on the spot. Very impressive.

The teacher that's with us today
Deserves all she gets for her pay.
I don't know her yet,
But I'm willing to bet,
She's got very thick skin, I'll say!

Half the class howled, slapping their thighs, and I suddenly knew why, not to mention the reason for my discomfort.

I felt behind me for the tack. It was packed to the hilt, all the way through my girdle, into me. Smiling, I surreptitiously removed Leonard's surprise, slipping it into an open drawer.

My First Year in the Classroom

"Good job, Leonard." I hoped he understood I meant the poem.

"What I would like you all to do with that paper I handed out is to write an autobiography, a short summary of your life. You can just touch on the highlights." I paused. "The sharpest memories."

Their smiles told me that my joke had sunk in.

As for myself, my memory of the tack incident would have been much sharper if not for my nearly impenetrable girdle!

It's All about the
Preparation

by Stephen D. Rogers

I WAS DETERMINED to be prepared when I stepped in front of my class for the first time.

Being only slightly older than the college students who'd be filling out the room, I still remembered how quickly a teacher was judged either a dynamo or a bore, and I didn't want to be labeled the latter.

Having my students running to the registrar's office waving drop/add forms on the first day of classes would not be good.

Knowing what I wanted to cover the first week, I sat at the kitchen table with a pad of paper and jotted the points I wanted to cover.

But what if I forget a supporting idea?

I flipped to a new sheet and wrote a detailed outline, the kind I'd always hated producing, drilling down to I.A.1.a.i. Deciding this was too complicated to assemble by hand, I switched to the computer.

Sent my masterpiece of structure to the printer.

The words snuggled against the left-hand border seemed so bald. What if I panicked and misread one?

I rewrote the outline using full sentences.

Sent that to the printer.

But the format still made the lecture seem choppy, and I wanted to come across as a natural speaker, a storyteller even. Reading this aloud, I'd simply sound abrupt.

I recast my lesson plan in narrative format. I started each paragraph with a topic sentence, followed by three supporting statements, a formula I could follow in my sleep.

Reading my prose aloud in front of the bathroom mirror, I almost did fall asleep.

I went back and built in transitions, a digression, a few jokes. I'd be the teacher they'd always wished they had, the teacher who made coming to class a joy.

And the best part? I was preparing a week's worth of lecture. That meant I'd be free to concentrate on student responses until next weekend.

I practiced reading my pages until I no longer lost my place.

Then I practiced reciting from memory, glancing down every paragraph or so to keep myself on track.

Were the jokes sprinkled too haphazardly?

I reorganized the lecture and reprinted.

Decided to go with a larger font and printed it again.

Maybe I should change the line spacing to reduce the risk of—no. Now I was just procrastinating.

Reminding myself what was at stake (dynamo or bore?), I resolved to read the lecture aloud at least five more times. After all,

It's All about the Preparation

I'd moved things around. I didn't want to miss some priceless nugget of information or—worse—repeat part of Monday's lecture on Thursday.

Back into the bathroom I went.

Smile at the mirror.

Go.

And so I went. And went. And went.

And went.

Went.

Given the extent of my preparation, this class was going to be performance art. First student to stand up and applaud was getting an A.

I showed up for class thirty minutes early so I could figure out whether I wanted to sit, stand against the desk, or pace.

Really, there was no need to be afraid. I knew the material cold. I had my delivery down cold. The ball of lead sitting at the bottom of my stomach: cold.

Enough. I was going to be fine.

In ones and twos, the students wandered into the room.

I wrote my name on the blackboard. Paused. Wrote that I drank my coffee black.

Nobody was smiling when I turned around.

That's okay. It was early. I wasn't smiling either. In fact, the only reason I didn't have a cup of coffee in my hand was I'd been up all night drinking pot after pot to calm myself.

In the light of day, I saw the problem with that plan, but last night I'd been too tired to think straight.

I counted students until there were as many of them as there were names on the enrollment report centered on my desk.

"Good morning. Welcome to Creative Writing." Should I have introduced myself? The very idea felt strange, especially with my name behind me in big block letters. This was a writing course. I could assume my students knew how to read. Couldn't I?

After clearing my throat, I lifted my lecture packet, and dropped my gaze to the opening paragraph. Without glancing up, or even pausing to breathe, I proceeded to plow through five days' worth of lecture, stopping only when I reached the end.

Stopping just before the end, actually. I still had the presence of mind not to wish them a good weekend.

Silence.

I finally looked up from my pages to see the class divided into three groups: those furiously taking notes, those looking at someone else's notes, and those sitting with mouths hanging open.

One of the last group tentatively raised her hand and asked, "Are we responsible for everything you said?"

"I realize that was a bit much, a bit fast," I said. I smiled, surprised to discover that even if it didn't reassure the class, it reassured me. "Don't worry, though. I'll be going over the main points until everybody has the theories down pat."

After all, I had nothing prepared for tomorrow.

It's All about the Preparation

Classroom Clown

by Marie Dixon Frisch

I DIDN'T MEAN to be a "nonconformist."

My first English class should have been perfect. I had analyzed the students' learning needs and prepared targeted exercises. The lesson was planned to the letter, with instructions scripted according to the model, and I had even jotted down jokes for in between. I'd prepared ten whole pages of work.

And then two jokers showed up, waltzing in at the last moment to throw me off.

"Two new students didn't make any difference," my supervisor criticized me later. "You should have followed the plan."

Yeah, right.

A couple of unknowns sauntered into the room two minutes before my English teaching debut, and burst my bubble of illusory control. I was tickled. I love it when the joke is on me.

By some fluke, I had lined up two extra chairs. But who were these people, and what did they want? An enquiring mind needed to know. I used the two minutes to get their names and find out a little about them.

When I registered for the intensive Certificate in English Language Teaching to Adults (CELTA) training course for teachers of English as a second language, the interviewer had warned me to take care of my physical and mental health. The course would be grueling. No problem, I thought. I adopted a vegetarian diet, increased my yoga and Qi Gong exercises, and got my husband to do the housework—hurray!

It was all for a good cause. I desperately needed a new source of income. I was tired of my lousy financial situation and wanted a "real" job that paid.

Our tutors were highly organized. They knew our weaknesses, our backgrounds, and interests. They often set up complicated "coincidences" to facilitate learning. The organizational corset was so tight, it was difficult to breathe, or even use the bathroom. You had to find a tutor when the toilet paper ran out.

Secretly, I rebelled against the ultra-organized structure. One colleague—a wonderful Canadian guy who'd served us fresh strawberries on a silver platter at lunch—dropped out like a swatted fly on the third day. I had to do something. But I didn't know what, until someone sent in the clowns.

The two students settled into their seats.

I looked at them and smiled. I was liberated. Still clutching my reams of notes, I abandoned the plan and let the lesson happen.

"My name," I told them, "is Marie."

I then spent ten minutes explaining different ways I'd learned to pronounce my name. I knew one student had trouble with the basics, even though she seemed fairly strong orally. My name was the only word I knew well enough to analyze phonetically. At the end of the class, the student I had meant to teach spelling and phonics confirmed that she'd learned all about the word Marie.

From the back of the room, my tutor signaled for me to move on.

So I did. I now wanted to demonstrate that there could be many ways of saying the same thing, while testing the learning styles and needs of my students. But everything seemed to go wrong. It took much longer than I had expected to get the words out.

The students stared at me as if I'd recently landed from Pluto.

Halfway through the lesson, I paused. I gazed at the silent, expectant faces and had no idea what to do next. Yet, it didn't seem to matter. Something beyond English language and my preconceived plan was going on in the classroom.

Had I gone mad? What was happening to me? It was my voice and my body at the front of the room, but my spirit was floating, enjoying the show. Despite the tension of the situation, I was encompassed by a cloud of calmness.

The feeling was rather nice.

At the end of the lesson, I smiled back at a stream of "mistakes." I'd taught the wrong emphasis on "variety," then corrected it. I'd told the Russian guy three ways of saying "I like vanilla ice cream," leaving him more confused than ever. I'd made the students look up names of foods, but neglected to correct their pronunciation.

The lesson must have seemed like a language-teaching disaster area. I had blown it. Magnificently.

Still . . .

My colleagues, observing from the back of the classroom, wore an aura of understanding. The students' faces were warm and contented. We'd sung the song about pronouncing tomato and potato—unheard of, one colleague marveled. I had debunked his belief that it was impossible to get adult German learners to sing.

I had become an instrument and the lesson had flowed through me. My mistakes proved that it was okay to be imperfect. We can all learn from each other. And no mistake is so terrible that we cannot either correct it, or learn from it and move on.

At least, that was what I concluded from my first day in the teaching arena.

My tutor, unimpressed, chided me for breaking the rules. I didn't know what rules she meant, but my mountain of mistakes probably reeked of anarchy to her.

I have always been a class clown. I am no less a clown for having chosen to become a teacher. I have a good chuckle whenever I think about my first lesson.

The students all came back, however, and their English eventually improved.

Nowadays, I write lesson plans with a lot less detail and a lot more space for the unknown. I know I am not in control.

And guess what else I know?

Clowns rule!

What Do You Teach Best?

by Felice Prager

WHEN I WAS SEARCHING for my first teaching position almost thirty years ago, the job market was padlocked against anyone without experience. With a just-out-of-college resume like mine, even getting an interview was considered a major accomplishment.

I was eager to start my career and determined to do it on my own. I sent out hundreds of resumes to schools around the state, a tedious process in the pre-computer era. When, after several months, I had received only one response, and that response asking if I'd work as an assistant secretary in a small elementary school, I decided to bury my pride.

One phone call to a family friend who knew someone who knew someone who knew someone earned me an interview with a superintendent of schools.

He drummed his fingers on the top of his desk. "Miss Prager, I only have three questions."

"Yes?"

"Can you create a sentence with a predicate adjective?"

"Yes. The superintendent of schools is nice." It wasn't a great example, but it was correct.

"If there is a teachers' strike, will you participate?"

While I didn't know if one was in the offing, I knew how to answer. "No, Sir. I would not participate in any strike ever."

Then the superintendent leaned back in his chair, put his hands behind his head, and said in a most personal and inviting manner, "Felice, what do you teach best?"

Finally, a real question. I created what I thought was a genuinely unique answer about how I taught reading best. I spoke for a long time, sounding to my own ears intelligent, informed, and dedicated.

When I finally finished, the superintendent lowered his arms, leaned forward, and announced with too much enthusiasm, "WRONG!"

I looked at him quizzically. How could such a profound answer be wrong?

"Here is the right answer. You teach CHILDREN best. Children. Everything else is gravy."

Then, as I stood, he scribbled on the bottom of my resume: "Female. No experience. Can't coach football."

So much for the family friend who knew someone who knew someone who knew someone.

Back I went to sending out resumes.

Eventually, I got my name on a list of substitute teachers in another town. I got my first contracted teaching position, one that lasted about a decade, when a teacher left her tenured position for a maternity leave and never came back.

During that time, I taught predicate adjectives and participated in three teacher strikes.

I taught literature. I taught grammar. I taught SAT verbal skills.

I taught reading. I taught mnemonic spelling tricks.

I taught my students how to write letters and how to give directions to their homes.

I taught students how to write reports and term papers.

I taught Latin and Greek prefixes and suffixes.

I taught students how to use a library, a dictionary, and a thesaurus.

On occasion, I taught manners.

I taught many students the reason why one doesn't put gum under a desk, lean back on two legs of a chair, or write on furniture.

In my newest position at a private multisensory education clinic, I work one-on-one with children who have a variety of "learning differences."

Parents come to our learning center desperately seeking help for their children. Many have tried everything within the schools to get assistance for their children. They've tried other tutoring facilities. They've tried reading books and searching the Internet for help.

We are often their last hope.

In our one-on-one facility, it is all about teaching the individual child.

One little girl started coming to the clinic last spring. She was in first grade and her parents realized there was something wrong when the teacher continually sent home notes saying that the student's behavior was poor.

The little girl couldn't sit still. She was disruptive and combative. She could not read the simplest words. She refused to even try.

According to her teacher, she seemed to exhibit mild signs of dyslexia. More important, she was a constant distraction in a class of twenty-nine other first graders.

A few afternoons a week, I worked with her on short words that have short vowel sounds. Doing so, I discovered she was creative and loved to draw things, especially animals. I incorporated that new knowledge into her curriculum.

One afternoon she came to see me, bubbling with excitement.

Her mother said, "Tell Felice what you just told me in the car."

"I raised my hand in class today and got the answer right."

That was a huge first step for her. Huge.

The next day I got a personal call from her first-grade teacher. "I don't know what you've done, but please don't stop!"

We chatted about how she wished she had the time to work with each child the way I can. "There's just so much to do. Strange as it sounds, a single child can't come first."

I totally understood. The clinic provided me with a luxury of time and resources that simply weren't available in a regular public school. That's why successes, when we had them, seemed so dramatic. We could focus on the children.

The other day, I met with the mother who wanted to interview me before enrolling her child. It's not uncommon.

She asked how the clinic worked.

I answered her.

She asked me what my credentials were.

I answered her.

Then she asked, "What do you teach best?"

I flashed back to that interview with the superintendent, oh so many years ago. He may have been condescending, but he'd had a valid point.

I smiled and answered, "I teach CHILDREN best."

I finally got the third answer right.

The First Day of the Rest of My Career

by Rosemary Troxel

AUGUST HAD LONG since passed, and only faint memories of graduation from Illinois State Teacher's College lingered in my mind. I was now focusing on my new career, a career I had practiced and longed for since I was old enough to sit in a chair and play school with my dolls and stuffed animals.

I lived at home with my mother. As I prepared for my first day at school, my mother priced billboards so she could announce to the world the fact that her daughter had gotten a job as a fourth-grade teacher in the town where we lived. Or perhaps that's just how it felt. "If your father had lived, he would have been so proud!"

After months of planning, the day arrived. I was a little lightheaded because I hadn't eaten much due to a bad case of nerves. My mother hugged and kissed me as I dashed out the door. I still remember her teary smile. I only hoped I wouldn't disappoint her.

Having arrived at school about an hour and a half earlier than the students, I had plenty of time to go over my lessons, reviewing my list of morning activities. I was anxious to meet some of my more "famous" students. I secretly giggled as I wondered whether "James Taylor" or "Gregory Peck" would look anything like their older namesakes.

Many of the other last names also were familiar, but only because I'd gone to school with their aunts and uncles, back in the day.

After what seemed like a lifetime, the bell finally rang, and I raced out to meet my students. Most were dressed in their Sunday best, their hair curled or styled with what looked like hair gel borrowed from Elvis's hairdresser.

By 10:00, the newness of the school year had already begun to wear off, and the children started to assume their true personalities.

Bradley, an adorable boy with a charming smile, announced, "You sure do look different than the picture my Uncle Frank showed me of you in high school! Do you wear contact lenses now?"

He was referring to my senior year photo. I'd worn a flip hairdo and black plastic glasses that formed a point on the outer edges of my face, not unlike like bat wings. It was somewhat stylish at the time, but in the present must have seemed like I'd been dressed for Halloween.

Perhaps there were downsides to teaching in one's hometown.

Several of the students, noticing my obvious embarrassment, scolded Bradley. While I appreciated their coming to my defense, I knew I needed to respond, and struggled for a way to turn this into a learning opportunity.

"Bradley," I said, "I was in high school four years ago. I am sure that if I were to look at a picture of you from four years ago, you might look a little different, too, don't you think?"

"Boy, that's for sure! I had missing teeth and hair that stuck out all over the place like a porcupine."

Other students joined in, excited to tell how funny they had looked at that time in their lives.

I held up my hand. "Boys and girls! I can tell by your enthusiasm that you all have stories to tell about how you looked when you were younger. Four years is a long time. That's a third of your life. We will ALL have a chance to draw a picture and write a story telling how we have changed in four years."

And so I learned a very valuable lesson on this first day of my teaching career. Seize the moment. Let the needs of the students drive instruction whenever possible. Let them see a purpose for learning. Let them crave it.

I walked around the room passing out blank paper. "Do you behave differently than you did four years ago? Do you look different? Do you like to do different things? Tell me all the ways you have changed since then. I will write my story, too."

After writing and illustrating our stories, we discussed the commonalities we shared. Although each of us was different, we learned that we all had awkward times in our lives. We all had sad times. We all had happy times.

That insight allowed the students to see each other in a new light. A new level of respect was reached.

This spontaneous event set the tone for how I taught that first year, and all that followed.

The First Day of the Rest of My Career

Sometimes my well-planned lessons had to take a backseat for more important issues.

Rather than practicing handwriting, we might need to talk about why a student's dog had been hit by a car. Maybe instead of playing "Around the World" to practice our math facts, we talked about how family "shapes" changed sometimes. The loss of a fellow student due to a parent's job move might supplant a week's curriculum.

Throughout it all, students learned the value of writing and journaling to process their thoughts and feelings. All of this began with that first day's writing project.

On the last day of school, I watched my "almost fifth graders" walk out of my classroom.

I couldn't imagine them looking back at pictures taken of them this day and feeling anything but pride. They were highly intelligent, fabulously considerate students, writers, and people. They were certainly taller than the beautifully dressed and coiffed students who had walked into my classroom nine months before.

We changed that year, all of us, a trend that continued as my first-year teaching became my second and third.

The Twisted, Noisy Path

by Diane Payne

BECAUSE I GRADUATED FROM college in December, my first day teaching was the day the students returned from winter break. They'd spent most of the first semester with substitute teachers, which didn't strike me as a point in my favor.

A month before, I'd spent a day with them. I'd been provided a lesson plan during my interview, and was expected to spend this introduction/trial day teaching. As if trying to teach a class of students after appearing in their fifth-grade classroom from out of nowhere wasn't hard enough, I had to do so in front of several frowning adults who were taking copious notes on my every comment and move.

I'd prepared all weekend, only to discover once I started that the lesson plan had been used the day before.

I glanced at the adults hunched over their clipboards, pens raised.

There was no help there.

Fortunately, I had brought some of my favorite books and somehow managed to keep the kids busy the entire day. I must have done well enough because I didn't receive any telephone calls over winter break telling me that a terrible mistake had been made.

I certainly gave the principal enough reasons to think that afterward.

This school had a strict Assertive Discipline policy that made the hallways seem unusually quiet. I'm not very quiet and I tend to run more than walk, so I had a hard time following all the school rules. As I was often reminded.

The teacher in the classroom next to mine would pull open the divider between us to discipline me for not keeping my class quiet. Most of the time I hadn't even noticed that we were being loud. It must have been strange for my students to see me getting in trouble, but maybe it helped us bond.

One day, while the kids were busy working in their science centers, two boys cleverly mixed some chemicals that should have been kept separate. Off went the smoke alarm and here came the fire department.

As we stood on the hot playground (we were located in the Mohave Desert), waiting for permission to re-enter the school, the teacher who loved to scold me for making too much noise just shook her head at me, with a look of disgust.

I took full blame for the science project disaster and refused to mention which students might have been involved. While I did this partly because I felt at fault, I also didn't want either boy in trouble. I'd seen how they were disciplined at home when one came in with a black eye.

So much for following the school's Assertive Discipline policy.

Not only did the two boys later apologize to me for their science experiment, they also asked to become my helpers. I'd been warned that these boys were bad, regulars at causing trouble, but now they were putting that behavior behind them.

It was a large class with close to forty students. The windowless room was so big that I had trouble seeing the kids at the back, and ended up getting glasses.

My favorite part of the day was recess. After all, I was bottled up in the classroom, too!

I was more than happy to go outside and play kickball, relieved to finally be able to make noise and run.

I started afterschool recreation programs where we'd play kickball, or I'd teach the kids how to fix their bikes, and then we'd go riding. Everyone walked or rode a bike to school, because there were no buses.

I'm sure people wondered when I'd burn out for spending so much free time with the kids, but I was young and energetic, and the only other person I knew in the town was my boyfriend.

While I'd moved a couple hundred miles to take this job and be near him, we could see just so much of each other without going crazy.

My boyfriend was the director of the local Child Protective Services. When I called CPS to report the boy with the black eye, I'm sure there was no doubt who made the call. So much for anonymity.

All things considered, school was going well. My students and I had learned to mostly whisper in class, I figured out how to quit dragging home all those horrible workbooks to grade each night, and the kids seemed to be enjoying school and their lessons.

The Twisted, Noisy Path

The learning centers I'd set up allowed the kids to work independently, which gave me more time to help the kids who benefited from individualized attention.

When that first year ended, I knew my students weren't going to get the great Iowa test scores that were sure to come to the students next door, but my students—and I—learned a lot. I'd attended their birthday parties and family dinners. If becoming involved with their lives made my students feel more comfortable, and school seem more amiable, then I was all for it. Happy children made good learners. That's why we were there, right?

The teacher next door to me would be horrified.

But that's what traveling the road to knowledge is like. Sometimes it's an empty four-lane highway, and sometimes it's a twisted, noisy path.

A First Year That Never Ended

by Dr. Bobby R. Ezell

TODAY I WORK AT a university preparing young teachers for the students they will someday teach. I have a voice from my first year of teaching that helps me with the task.

The place was Aldine Junior High School, the un-air-conditioned learning edifice for 700 sixth-, seventh-, and eighth-grade students in 1966. That year the AJH administration offered me my first teaching job. I was twenty-two.

The voice belongs to Kathleen.

My teaching schedule included three sections of seventh-grade English. This was a time in our educational history when all students were academically grouped with overt titles identifying each class section. The smart kids were in section 7-1, the slower ones were in 7-15, and the others were stuck somewhere in between. The counselors denied that the numbers referred to academic ability, but the teachers knew the truth, and so did the students.

I taught sections 7-3, 7-7, and 7-8. There were more than thirty-five fourteen-year-old boys and girls in each section. Each daily class meeting was two hours long. I was responsible for teaching two subjects during the two hours, English and reading. At the end of each six-week grading period, I was responsible for giving each student a grade in each of the subjects.

Kathleen was in section 7-8, a group of kids identified as being exactly in the middle of the academic range. She was a skinny kid with long, stringy, dishwater-blonde hair. Her sparkly brown eyes were a part of her smile.

I liked the kid. She was zany. She obviously liked school, was a little boy crazy, and often giggled when she addressed me.

Whenever she asked me a question in class, Kathleen would intentionally mispronounce my name. She'd say, "Mr. Eschell, what do you think about . . . ?" She'd then follow the question with her mouth-and-eyes combination smile.

Her grades were fairly good. I heard from other teachers that her home life was difficult, but she kept up on her schoolwork. I noted that her parents did not attend open house, but I never got involved enough to learn more about her situation.

As my first year of teaching ended, so ended any contact with Kathleen.

During my second year, I heard that Kathleen was dating a boy who had dropped out of high school. At midterm, a teacher mentioned to me that Kathleen had dropped out of school and married.

I didn't think about Kathleen again until May of my third year of teaching. It was then that I read in a Houston newspaper about a young sixteen-year-old suicide victim who had killed herself during a quarrel with her young husband.

The victim's name was Kathleen.

She was the same Kathleen.

I was outraged. I was not prepared for such a mean, hateful, sad event to be a part of my teaching experience. I thought that my role was to teach students to appreciate short stories and poetry, and to get them to write their reactions to literary pieces.

When I decided to become a teacher, I never dreamed that one of my students would commit suicide. I never thought that such a horrendous deed would create the need for me to re-examine all that I was doing and the way I was doing it.

After Kathleen's death, I thought back many, many times about the year she spent with me in seventh-grade English. "When she was in my class, did I do enough to make her feel she was important? Did I speak to her when I saw her in the hallway?"

After her death, when I looked at her grades in the grade book, I asked, "Were these grades that I wrote down in my grade book and gave to Kathleen each six weeks the only message that I sent telling her what I felt she was as a person?"

I was there to make a difference in the lives of young people. Had I failed?

This year, I'm beginning my forty-fourth year as a teacher. I still have that grade book.

The students who were in section 7-8 are today around fifty-five years old. Many of them are probably grandparents. When I reflect about that time, I think about Kathleen, and when I do, she is always a fourteen-year-old seventh grader with stringy blonde hair and shiny brown eyes that complement her smile.

And in my reflection, she admonishes me, "Mr. Eschell, teach these young teachers that they must make their students know that they care about them. Teach these young teachers that their future students need so much more than a grade on a report card. You make sure you do that, Mr. Eschell. Okay?"

A Class Surprise

by Gail Carter Johnson

THE FIRST TIME I saw the high school library with its rich golden wood, wide windows, and row after row of shelves, I fell in love. Even the work area was sufficient, except that the desk belonging to the old librarian took up so much space. I asked, "When is Mrs. Crawford moving to the main office?"

Principal Simpson shrugged. "Soon."

As the principal left, Mrs. Crawford joined me. She seemed nice enough, but this was my library now.

Mrs. Crawford handed me a sheet of paper.

"What's this?" I scanned the list of twenty-four names.

"Why, Gail, I thought you knew. The names are your homeroom."

"Homeroom?"

"Yes, it's customary for the second librarian to have one."

"Second librarian?"

What a dreadful start. My first position came with a homeroom, an aged librarian who seemed determined to watch me like a hawk, and twenty-four kids who would probably just sit there and judge.

I started memorizing the names.

Was Liz nice? Tony? Debbie?

How many were good students? How many were troublemakers?

My students slowly wandered in, took their chairs, and stared at me.

What were they thinking? Did I look old enough? Did I look like a librarian, but not so much like a librarian that I could be mistaken for Mrs. Crawford?

I called the roll from memory. Their expressions changed when I called their names, as if I knew all their sins and redeeming qualities.

Mrs. Crawford walked around the perimeter of the room like a guard, or the ghost of a guard, doomed to haunt this patch of land forever.

I shook the thought from my head and read the announcements. Then I dismissed for first period. I breathed a sigh of relief until I noticed that Liz and Debbie were still sitting there.

"Girls, aren't you supposed to go to class?"

In unison they replied, "First period's study hall. We decided to be library helpers."

"Library helpers." Was this Mrs. Crawford's idea? Maybe another way to spy on me? "Perhaps you'd like to shelve new books."

"New books!" Debbie sounded excited.

Liz glanced around. "I thought Mrs. Crawford went to the main office. You are the librarian, aren't you?"

"Yes, Liz, I am. Mrs. Crawford will be moving soon."

"Good."

I let the remark pass, and showed the girls what I needed them to do. That was the high point of my week.

The rest of the time, Mrs. Crawford was telling me what she wanted me to do. Perhaps Mr. Simpson hadn't told her I'd been hired to run the library.

I discovered that I enjoyed having a homeroom and dealing with the students. I suggested books they might find interesting, and they offered up personal tidbits. The students were certainly more fun to have around than Mrs. Crawford.

While we eventually formed a professional relationship, I wanted her gone. Even the purse sitting on her desk felt like a slap in the face.

I focused on the students: teaching library classes, training assistants, and helping with research.

A month passed. Mr. Simpson summoned me to his office. "Gail, I know I told you Mrs. Crawford was moving to the main office."

"Yes, I was wondering what was taking so long."

"She doesn't want to go. The superintendent is backing her up." His phone rang. "I can fight only so many battles. I'm sure you understand."

When he answered the phone, I stood and staggered from his office. Mrs. Crawford wasn't moving? Was I the librarian or not?

Six weeks passed. Coexisting with Mrs. Crawford remained difficult, and that pocketbook of hers seemed to grow larger and larger until it filled the entire work area. How soon before that purse filled the entire library, my whole life? I think Mrs. Crawford had more than a passing acquaintance with certain works of one Edgar Allan Poe.

Finally, it was time for report cards. Students with overdue materials couldn't get their report cards until they rectified the situation,

A Class Surprise

and although I had sent reminders and talked to many of the students on the list, not all had produced the materials they'd borrowed.

Seventy students formed a line that wound outside the library and they buzzed with angry voices.

Fortunately, Liz and Debbie were available to help. They handled the students who were paying their fines. I handled the students who wanted to argue.

Slowly, the line dwindled, but the noise and confusion grew worse. As my students started raising their voices, I warned them several times to keep it down, all to no avail.

Enough was enough.

"Everybody freeze! Quiet!"

As the room was shocked into silence, I heard the buses outside.

"Nobody is released."

The students fidgeted. Squirmed. Rolled their eyes.

I held firm.

This was my library. I was in charge.

Students glanced out the windows, worry starting to show on their faces.

Deciding I'd made my point, I let them go.

They burst out of the room like Olympians.

The next day, nobody said a word. I took attendance silently, read the announcements, and dismissed them for first period.

Liz and Debbie approached me. "Where's Mrs. Crawford?"

For the first time that morning, I realized Mrs. Crawford wasn't in the library. I checked the work area. Neither was her purse.

Then I saw the note on my desk. "You're ready. Gone to main office. Call if you ever want to chat."

Maybe she knew a thing or two after all.

Lessons Learned

by Nancy Kelly Allen

I HOPE I CAN. I hope I can. I hope I can.

The mantra echoed through my mind as I climbed up the two long, steep sets of stairs to the eighth-grade classroom where twenty-five students would soon greet me on my first day of school.

For the students, half of their school year was complete. I was their third teacher that year. Should I feel charmed or alarmed?

As I was young and innocent, I looked at the positive side of life and chose to feel charmed, until the students walked through the door. Some were a foot taller and seventy pounds heavier than me.

The principal introduced me in a no-nonsense manner and privately advised, "Don't show your pearly whites in a smile until the last day of school, and keep the students busy."

I looked around the classroom at the students. The students looked at me. None looked as nervous as I felt. After introductions, I set them to work silently reading a chapter on the Civil War in their history books. The silence lasted almost as long as the BB-size cough drop in my mouth.

I must have said "Quiet" more often than all the Civil War generals together said "Charge!"

One student walked into the classroom about fifteen minutes after class had started.

I asked, "Where have you been?"

"I was confused," he said, his voice dripping with mock apology. "I thought we had PE and I went to the gym by mistake."

"I see," I said, not seeing at all, especially as he looked around and grinned at his friends. Muffled laughter coursed around the classroom.

That afternoon, so many students needed to use the restroom so many times, I thought an outbreak of a bladder virus had swept through the school.

I survived that first day, but it was the longest seven hours of my life. Sure, I had diplomas. Sure, I had the requisite student teaching experience. Sure, those and pocket change would buy me a cup of coffee.

I quickly learned the names of my students, but more important, I gradually learned the students.

One day, I noticed that an outgoing student was unusually quiet. During class I eased over to him and asked if he was feeling well. He shrugged. I could hear the heartbeat of disappointment in his body language. A few minutes later he told me his father left home and he was afraid his parents would divorce.

Every day at 12:30, we got down to the serious business of lunch. I always sat with my students in the cafeteria. When we were there, we set aside class work, discipline problems, and all things school.

Those moments fueled rich personal discussions. We chatted about issues of interest to each of us: the delicious chicken on our plates, a hit song by Rod Stewart, a new baby brother for one, a new home for another, a divorce, or a remarriage. Most of the discussions were low-key and packed with humor. Humor was the universal language that every student understood.

I declared the last hour of the last Friday of each month Special Friday. Special Friday was a time for students to showcase their talents. Many chose to take advantage of the venue, but some did not. The students surprised me more often than not.

Personalities evolved and transformed—from shy to bold, from daring to timid—within the same student as situations changed.

A gregarious young girl clammed up tighter than a banjo string when her best friend tried to get her to perform a short skit.

The friend looked at me. "Miss Allen, tell her she'll do fine."

I looked at the young lady who had suddenly turned shy and decided to give encouragement through humor. "Performing in front of your first audience is like kissing your first mule," I said. "It's better if—"

Before I could finish the sentence, another student called out, "You kiss it quick."

Humor worked its magic. The young lady laughed, stood, and portrayed her character. Nervousness created a few stumbles and a blush or two, but her friends turned a blind eye to her blunders and praised her performance.

An introverted young man, who I thought might never participate, suspended his shyness the first day as he took center stage and sang his favorite song. The class applauded, and he stood a little taller as he walked back to his seat.

Another trick I used was that each day after lunch, I read a chapter from a book. Even the most restless, inattentive students sat as quiet as a mouse, and listened. We followed each reading with a discussion of the characters and the plot and made predictions of what would happen next.

One day, a student who first alarmed me charmed me by asking if I would like to have a puppy—a terrier mix—and I answered without thinking. "I'd love to have four little paws running around my house."

The next day, a Friday, I brought home my little bundle of joy, wrapped snugly in a washcloth, and named him "Chopper."

Monday morning, I made the big announcement about the new addition to my family. Every day, students wanted to hear more about my little dog. Every day, I told about what he had chewed up or barked at. Every day, they laughed at his antics and enjoyed the up-close-and-personal insight into my life.

That first year of teaching saw many lessons learned. By some strange twist, sometimes I was the student, and my students my teachers. Even Chopper got in some lessons for me, which shouldn't be a surprise to anyone who's ever owned a puppy.

Jeremy, Jeremy, Jeremy

by Albert W. Caron, Jr.

THE FIRST TIME I saw Jeremy, he stood out in a crowd of nervous students. He was five foot eight, a bit taller and heftier than most eighth graders, and anything but nervous looking.

Jeremy also stood out because he was the only student wearing a baseball cap inside the building. And backwards at that. As it was the first day after summer break, I figured this kid was "forgetting the rules" in an attempt to get a rise.

Now seemed to be the perfect time to set the record straight, to prove that this new teacher wasn't a pushover.

I was sauntering over to where Jeremy was standing when the principal stopped me. "Jeremy can wear the hat. He has a medical excuse, scalp condition."

"Oh, okay." I let it go.

A bit later I received the roster for my homeroom and classes. The kid with the backward hat, Jeremy, was on it. I not only had him for homeroom but also for English.

My gut told me we were going to have issues. I could see it plain as day, just by the way I saw him standing there earlier.

It wasn't long before my suspicions were justified.

Jeremy would come to class unprepared two or three times per week, conveniently forgetting his pen, pencil, notebook, agenda, assignment, and so on. In a few weeks he was staying after school for these discipline infractions.

"Jeremy, Jeremy, Jeremy," I asked, hearing the exasperation in my voice, "where are you planning to go next year?"

He indicated a vocational technical school.

I told him that was great, and asked what he was going to study.

He didn't know.

"It doesn't matter, really." I took a deep breath, trying to figure out how best to reach him, "Success in any endeavor boils down to some very simple facts. You have to be responsible. Right now, you have to bring your materials to class every day. Not just when you want, but every day. You're going to have to be just as responsible at the vocational technical school. And when you later have a job as an electrician, plumber, or carpenter, you'll have to be responsible then. If you don't bring your equipment to the job site, you won't be able to work."

Jeremy nodded.

I didn't know whether he listened, whether he was just signaling that he'd heard me, or whether he was keeping the beat to a song playing in his head, but for a few short weeks, the situation improved.

Then he was back to his old self, "forgetting" his pen or pencil or assignment.

He blew off my detention and received an office detention. I asked that he be assigned to my room so I could counsel him again, but this time Jeremy ignored all my efforts at dialogue.

"Fine," I said. "Just sit there. If you don't want to do this every day until school gets out, come to class prepared. Otherwise, you're going to have to face the consequences of your actions."

So the year went. Jeremy remembered for a while. Then he "forgot" for a while.

I wasn't experienced enough to know any other approaches. The teachers I asked just shrugged, "Jeremy." As if that was an answer.

Fast-forward to May, a month before eighth-grade graduation. I had surgery and missed the end of school, including the promotion exercises.

Jeremy, I was told later, wore a brand-new hat that day—backwards, of course!

Because I missed that last month, I felt as though my first year had ended with unfinished business. I didn't have closure with any of my students, but Jeremy . . . Jeremy was like an itch I couldn't scratch.

Would those few weeks have made any difference? Could I have made him understand? Sometimes a year isn't enough.

The following October, I was dealing with a fresh crop of students.

I had my back to the class and I was writing on the board when I heard someone tapping a pen incessantly on a desk. Without looking back, I said, "Knock it off."

The drumming continued.

Frustrated, I put the chalk down before turning.

There was Jeremy sitting in a chair at the rear of the class. He continued to tap his pen, a huge grin on his face. "I remembered it!"

"Jeremy! How are you?" I felt my own face light up.

"I came back to say hi. I missed you at the end of last year. How are you feeling?"

I updated Jeremy on my recovery as I walked over to shake his hand.

"I also wanted to thank you for pushing me. I got in trouble up at voc-tech," Jeremy admitted sheepishly. "I wasn't prepared for class and, man, they were all over me. I remembered what you said."

I playfully removed his hat and mussed the hair I'd seen growing out every which way. "I hope it's finally beginning to sink in." I tapped his head.

We smiled at each, and then he stood. He'd grown even taller, and leaner, than I remembered him. "Well, I have to go, Mr. Caron, but I wanted to thank you."

With that, he gave me a bear hug, and before leaving the room told my students, "He's the man."

Another teacher who'd had Jeremy saw him leave my room, and asked, "What was that all about?"

When I explained, I thought her jaw was going to hit the floor. "Wow."

"Yes, wow." That's all I could say, too, standing there with a huge grin on my face, a lump in my throat, the hint of a tear in my eye. Wow.

Sometimes the first year just takes a little longer.

We Are Just Crazy

by Yuria R. Orihuela

SINCE I ALWAYS PLAYED school as a child, and I loved mathematics, it only made sense for me to become a math teacher.

First, I needed my materials.

The day before school started, I was taken to a dark, cramped room containing piles of what looked like books that had gone through a hurricane or two.

"Pick what you want."

"For what?"

"You're teaching the low students. These will be good enough."

"Are you sure?" I leaned toward one of the piles, trying not to touch anything until I had to.

"The senior teachers get the good books. It's a simple matter of privilege."

"But—"

"If you can't find enough books that are usable, you can always supplement."

Supplement? I didn't even know how to implement!

Gritting my teeth, I started going through the piles, pulling out any book that did not have any "moving parts." Materials? Check. Sort of.

Second, I needed my students.

The next day I got them, and I could tell by the looks on their faces that they were thinking, "We're going to have fun with this one." "This one" meaning me.

Third, I needed some idea of how to manage students who would rather interact with their friends in the classroom than their teacher. I'd been given three pieces of advice: keep them busy, be strict so that they know you mean business, and don't smile until Christmas.

That last piece of advice seemed about as valuable as the textbooks I'd been given. How could I not smile? I loved school, I loved math, and I loved young people. Now that I had all three, I was supposed to frown?

Of course some days, I was given reason to. I'll never forget when one male student grabbed and throttled another student. I sent for the assistant principal, but by the time he arrived, the two students were acting like best friends. The assistant principal spoke to the two boys in a calm, firm, and positive way.

When I saw how he commanded respect, I began to handle my classes differently. Little by little, things improved.

Just as I was beginning to feel that measurable progress was being made, I was told that due to low enrollment, I had to move to another school. "Take a few days to learn the school and the students before you start."

That seemed thoughtful. Only later did I learn that they needed those few days to create my classes. Worse, they created my classes by asking the other teachers to select the four students they most wanted out.

I was a floater. That meant I got to push my cart of materials through crowded halls of teenagers, trying desperately to reach my next assigned room on time and intact.

When I tried to appeal to the principal, my concerns were shunted aside. Students later told me the principal didn't want anything to do with members of the faculty or staff, except for one cute counselor. Supposedly, the two spent many hours behind locked doors discussing curriculum.

Finally, halfway through the year, a portable classroom that I might be able to use became available.

I was told I could have it, with two caveats. First, I would have to clean it (remove the numerous stacks of old newspapers and accompanying Florida insects). Second, I would now have to teach five different levels (basic, regular, and grades seven, eight, and nine) in one year.

I didn't know that the second condition was a violation of the union contract.

What I did know was that when I finally arrived home at the end of the day, I collapsed into bed and cried myself to sleep at least three times a week.

I felt as though the students did not want to learn, the teachers did not want to help me, and the administrators did not want to care.

Or maybe I wasn't cut out to teach.

That seemed true when I gave a test to my ninth-grade "basic" students and the grades were dismal. But then I noticed, on the side of one of the papers, a sprawl of awkward handwriting.

"Mrs. O, we do love you, we are just crazy."

I kept that piece of paper for years. It was that note that lifted my spirits and taught me what teaching was all about. That note took me back to my own years as an adolescent, the games we played, the pranks we attempted.

Students knew I was trying to teach them, but they had to have fun. They were children struggling with math concepts, not machines that could be programmed.

Don't smile until Christmas? I needed to smile every day. I needed my students to smile every day.

That simple note, scrawled on a test paper, turned my teaching career around.

Things didn't improve instantly. I had to try things, keep what worked, dump what failed. I had to develop a plan then tinker it.

At the end of that first school year, I received many similar notes from my students, notes that kept me going through the dark times.

I did not know if any of my students would become a mathematician or even a math teacher, but I knew that many would be going into the world with at least a smidgen of my love for mathematics.

And my smile—that I gave them all.

Part-Time Teaching Is a Full-Time Job

by Michelle Blackley

BEING HIRED AS a part-time faculty member at a local college, I was more than a little nervous at the thought of actually stepping in front of a classroom.

While I may have been twenty-nine, I could easily pass for the average underclassman. Would my students take me seriously? How about the other teachers? The administration?

Although I'd been hired, I wasn't so sure I was the right person for the job.

Nevertheless, armed with my master's degree and limited teaching experience, I was allowing myself to be thrown into the lion's den, a summer class of what I expected to be non-traditional students.

Will they "know" more than me? I knew it didn't take a degree to make people intelligent, especially if they had "real world" experience, and my class was teaching non-majors how to conduct a proper analysis of the media.

Everybody knew how to watch television. Most people knew how to read newspapers. What made me more of an expert than my students?

I dreaded the first night of class.

With all the doubts that fought for attention, I felt like a bundle of nerves. Just imagining myself standing in front of a lecture hall that seated ninety was enough to make me cower in a corner.

I was going to have to march up there and recite the syllabus. Not only that, I was going to have to return to the lecture hall again and again until I'd spewed four weeks' worth of material.

I felt like sending a note to my prospective students: "Since you're smart and dedicated enough to sign up for a summer course, you're smart and dedicated enough to make up your own mind regarding the media. Stay home and analyze."

Several deep breaths later, I came to my senses.

I was a teacher, and stepping in front of a classroom—or a lecture hall seating ninety—was what teachers did.

So I did it.

Now, more than a year into my teaching career, I still double- and triple-check my bag the night before. While I know what I plan to say, I also recognize that the class may develop differently. Students ask questions and give feedback. Despite the best intensions, some lessons fail.

When I wrote the syllabus, I couldn't include breaking news that wouldn't happen for three weeks, but students always wanted to talk about how the media was handling things as the situation unfolded.

Sometimes I felt as though I spent twenty-four hours a day watching every news broadcast, reading every newspaper and magazine, just to stay ahead of my students. I felt like I needed to be prepared enough so that whenever a student asked, "Did you read that story?" I could not only answer in the affirmative, but also have an educated analysis ready.

Being a novice teacher, I learned as much as my students that first year. They learned how to analyze the media. I learned how to balance acceptance and discipline.

Acceptance allowed mutual respect, a necessity before the class could be interactive and fun. Discipline allowed the syllabus and requirements to be met. I experimented that first year to find the perfect balance.

And I experimented with every class afterward, since every group of students required a different touch.

While I threw surprise quizzes and assigned impromptu speeches, the students still managed to surprise me more often than I managed to surprise them.

The biggest surprises were the compliments. The first time a student asked me to be her advisor, I didn't know what to say. Students also asked for recommendations to study abroad, as if I knew them well enough to be a judge. As for the stellar reviews, such as telling the department head I deserved a raise, well, they made me laugh as much as smile.

I was pleased—no, scratch that—ecstatic to read in the course evaluation how much the students learned. I was flattered when they asked what other courses I taught so they could take them.

A different type of surprise was actually more of a pleasure, and that was watching the students improve and grow.

One student, in Introduction to Oral Communications, spoke hesitantly about attending this college so that she could be near her boyfriend. The two broke up not long after the semester started, which served as the topic of her second speech, delivered with a bit more assurance. By the end of the course, she was telling us how she planned to move some 5,000 miles away, confident in tone as well as action.

Few things were more exciting to me than being able to watch students learn to think analytically for themselves.

Sweet Success

by Helen Lieberstein Shaphren as told to *Susanne Shaphren*

MY FIRST YEAR in the classroom was also my first year away from home. I eagerly looked forward to a bathroom I didn't have to share (in the apartment, not the school) and not having to eat my mother's creamed spinach.

After a few short weeks in Des Moines, I would have happily shared the bathroom in my St. Louis home with the population of China. I was so homesick I picked up that dreaded creamed spinach in the school cafeteria and ordered it at the nearby diner every lunch and dinner for weeks.

I'd always known I wanted to be a teacher. When my older brother and younger sister refused to play school, I arranged my dolls and teddy bears into neat rows and taught them instead. At least I could pretend they were good listeners.

Unlike so many of my friends who changed their career goals as they grew older, I never wavered from my desire to teach except for a brief period of time when I thought I wanted to become a doctor.

Nobody was surprised when I became a teacher, but family and friends raised their eyebrows when they learned my chosen specialty: working with deaf students. Firmly believing it was vital for deaf students to be able to understand and communicate with everyone they encountered, I continued my training at Central Institute for the Deaf (CID).

In the 1940s it was very modern and more than a bit controversial to have hearing teachers training deaf students how to read lips and speak, instead of deaf teachers instructing them how to sign.

Smouse Institute in Des Moines, Iowa, gave me the opportunity to put what I'd learned at CID to practical use.

While I'd worked with individual students during my training, this was my first class.

The skill levels of the students varied widely. A few of my students could read lips proficiently, and others barely at all.

I worked long and hard to bring the less skilled to a satisfactory level. I turned my face to the side or partially covered my lips to mimic what they would encounter in the world. Then we practiced, practiced, and practiced some more until all of the students had mastered this vital skill.

Another challenge was dealing with deaf students who interpreted language a bit too literally. One day, a little girl in the class asked why I looked so sad. I answered that a famous person had died.

"No!" she protested as though I was the student who needed to be taught. "He's not dead. He's out standing in his field. I read it in the newspaper. Where's his field?"

When I tried to incorporate slang into our daily language lessons to ease the transition to regular classes, I encountered similar problems. The common 1940s phrase "What's cooking?" caused one little boy to sniff and answer, "Soup!"

With patience, persistence, and creativity, I helped my students make significant progress in terms of comprehending and appropriately using language.

That left the even bigger challenge of keeping my students motivated enough to repeat speech drills until anybody could understand exactly what they were saying.

I knew that the long-term success of being mainstreamed into regular classrooms and never needing an interpreter would be worth every bit of effort—theirs and mine—but the kids needed a shorter-term goal to aim for, and a much more tangible reward.

My salary barely covered rent and other expenses, but I decided to spend part of it on weekly field trips to a nearby ice cream parlor.

I explained to my students that if they worked really hard on speech drills, they could order an ice cream cone every Friday afternoon. They quickly learned that if the lady behind the counter couldn't clearly understand what they asked for, she would scoop up and serve them vanilla (which none of my students liked).

One little boy cried when he didn't get the chocolate ice cream that he so desperately wanted, but I knew enough to remain firm.

Even though he was hardly one of my eager students, he suddenly started paying rapt attention to lessons. He worked harder and harder, especially during speech drills. I tried every creative tool I could think of to help him learn.

Despite our best efforts, he still wound up with the vanilla ice cream he hated.

Week after week.

Month after month.

Both of us stubbornly refused to give up.

Sweet Success

We practiced and we drilled.

Some days it seemed as though he got it. And then the next, whatever progress he'd made melted like a scoop of ice cream dropped on hot pavement.

We practiced and we drilled.

The school year was almost over. Would he ever taste success?

And then the day arrived when he was ready.

That little boy confidently approached the glass case and placed his order with perfectly understandable words. "Chocolate ice cream, please."

A lump rose in my throat as I watched him stand there, patiently waiting.

Then, when he finally got that special chocolate ice cream cone, the one he'd worked so very hard to earn, the only tears in the room were shed by me and the lady behind the counter.

Success never tasted as sweet as it did that first year in the classroom.

Helen Lieberstein Shaphren passed away in 2004, but her legacy lives on in the deaf students she taught to thrive independently in the hearing world long before scientists invented cochlear implants. After that first year in the classroom, my mother and her new husband moved west.

The state superintendent of public instruction barely glanced at her resume before telling her there was no need for special education in Arizona. He tossed her an application and said she could teach in any of his regular classrooms. She tossed the application back at him and pioneered oral education for the deaf in Arizona by starting a school in her home!

How to Teach When You Look Sixteen

by Rachel Garlinghouse

I'D ALWAYS LOOKED young for my age, which had sometimes worked to my advantage. Now that I was going to teach college students, however, I saw a definite drawback to my having the appearance of a high school sophomore.

My friends joked that I should walk into my classroom on the first day and sit at one of the student desks. Then, when it was time for class to begin, I could stand up, take my place at the lectern, and watch as eyes widened in shock.

I wasn't that brave. Or maybe I was brave enough not to play games but address the issue directly.

If I was going to command respect, I simply needed to look older than my students.

Purchasing fake glasses would make me appear intelligent and authoritative.

Wearing knee-length skirts and dress blouses would give me a professorial air.

I would cut my hair, wear conservative lipstick, and proudly carry a heavy, black briefcase.

Yes, and I would have them address me by my last name. That would surely demand respect.

That first day of the semester, I was terribly nervous. I got up too early after a night of restless sleep and found myself pacing the apartment in an attempt to burn off energy and minutes. Finally, the clock struck a reasonable time, and I headed to school, blaring upbeat, fast-paced music.

I pulled into the teacher parking lot, checked and rechecked my mascara in the visor mirror, and began the short trek to my building.

Had I remembered everything?

I was wearing a sleeveless gauzy white blouse and a knee-length pale pink flowing skirt. Mid-heeled dress sandals adorned my feet, and an artistic floral pendant hung around my neck. I wore my hair down and curled under (despite the humid, Midwest summer day).

The contents of my "teacher bag" had been carefully arranged and rearranged.

I hovered outside the classroom door for nearly ten minutes, shifting my weight uncomfortably in my heels, finally dialing my husband's cell phone number in a desperate bid for his assurance and good wishes.

After I hung up with him, I took a deep breath and entered the room, my heart pounding.

Inside, twenty-three expectant sets of eyes gave me the once-over, and then the twice-over. A few of the boys smirked and nudged one another. A few agreeable female students smiled politely and sat up straighter in their desks, their notebooks already opened and pens in hand.

Some students frowned in disbelief, while others just glanced away.

I hobbled over to the desk at the front of the room and gratefully put down my heavy bag. I smiled weakly at the students. "Good morning."

A few less-than-enthusiastic mumbles came back to me in reply.

I pulled out the attendance sheet and focused intently on words I wasn't reading.

Now what?

I felt sweat form on my chest and back as I tried to calm my pounding heart and bring my racing mind under control.

Too loudly, I said, "My name is Mrs. Garlinghouse, and this is English 101."

The students blinked.

Now what?

I had to draw a deep breath; focus on my teaching outline full of its bullet points and underlines.

I wasn't going to earn any respect from my students no matter how old I looked if I just stood up here and said nothing.

I was a teacher. I should be teaching.

Perhaps I should announce my name again, just in case somebody missed it.

Perhaps I should take attendance. Yes, that sounded like a good thing to do. It's very teacher-like.

I took attendance, and then the rest of the day is a blank.

While I followed my outline, time flew by in a blur, and I seem to have blocked the whole experience out of my mind, the way people do after they live through a disaster.

All I remember is leaving the building at the end of the day.

How to Teach When You Look Sixteen

On my way back to my car, I felt blisters beginning to form on the tops of my feet. My blouse clung to my sweating body, my bag made me lean unnaturally to one side, and my hair hung limply.

When I finally reached my car, I hit the unlock button and threw my black bag into the backseat with a bit more oomph than was necessary, happy to rid myself of its weight.

Then I started the engine, turned the music up loud, and headed home.

How you teach when you look sixteen is not much different from how you teach when you look sixty, or forty-seven.

Since that first day, I've taught sixteen composition courses to more than 300 college freshmen.

Just in case you're wondering, a typical day at work sees me dressed comfortably in wide-legged linen pants, a cotton top, and sandals. I wear my hair in a ponytail, and my makeup is minimal. I only wear glasses if my contact lenses are aggravating my allergies, and when I carry student essays, I do so in a beach bag.

I still don't look my age, but now my confidence comes from experience, not from my outward appearance.

Teaching Josh

by Mindy Hardwick

THE FIRST DAY of school, Josh arrived in my seventh-grade language arts class and proceeded to reach his seat by walking across the desks. He stepped up onto the chair nearest the door, and then, using the desks as a set of stepping stones, walked across the tops to the back of the room.

I stood with my mouth open. My principal had stressed the importance of taking charge of the classroom by setting a positive tone. Trying to recover from my shock, I said in my very best teacher voice, "Josh, you'll need to re-enter the classroom."

My heart pounded. Would he do as I asked? If he didn't, what did I do next?

It was the very first day of my first year teaching, and already I'd lost control.

Josh stepped off his desk and strolled past me to the door. When he reached the door, Josh turned around and walked back in. "Sorry," he said to me in the most remorseful voice I had ever heard, and then headed for his desk with his head down.

At that moment, I was hooked on this kid with the thick, shaggy blond hair, which usually hung into his bright blue eyes.

During the first weeks of September, Josh managed to keep himself mostly in check. "The honeymoon period," more experienced teachers said to me. "Wait until October."

I didn't have to wait that long.

By mid-September, it was painfully obvious that Josh could not sit still.

He was always out of his seat.

I would find him walking around the room or talking to another student. Over and over, I would remind Josh to sit down, to raise his hand if he wanted to talk, or to turn in a homework paper. And over and over, Josh would apologize for something that I was beginning to suspect was much bigger than he was.

When I asked the other teachers what might be wrong with Josh, they shook their heads and said, "Attention Deficit Disorder. His mom doesn't want him to be on medicine."

"What do I do?" I asked. This situation was not one for which I'd been trained. Surely Josh's aimless inability to concentrate couldn't go on all year.

"Give him detention," the other teachers said. "It doesn't help the ADD, of course, but you can't let him continue to get away with the disruptive behaviors. It teaches the other kids they can do the same things without consequence."

I hated to give Josh detention for something that seemed so much out of his control, but I knew the other teachers were right. Already, some of the other kids were starting to grumble about favoritism.

When Josh was out of his seat, I gave him a reminder. When other kids were out of their seats, I gave them detentions.

I wanted to tell them, no, it isn't fair, but neither is ADD.

In our school, the principal believed that detention was best served with the teacher who gave it. That way, the thirty-minute detention gave the student a chance to get to know the teacher on an individual basis, and at the same time the teacher was given an extra set of hands for preparing the next day's lessons.

As a first-year teacher, I spent long hours in my classroom preparing and correcting. I therefore enjoyed having the company of my seventh-grade students serving after-school detention, and tried to make the experience as positive as possible for everybody concerned.

Once Josh began serving detentions, I quickly discovered that he liked being helpful. He was also handy with repairing things.

"I can fix that," Josh would say, pointing to bookshelves that sagged, or desks that had lost a screw, or chairs with loose legs. And the next afternoon, he would appear with screws or small tools, eager to be helpful.

Although I found Josh to be childlike and charming, not all the teachers enjoyed his antics. By winter, the other teachers were tired of Josh's un-medicated ADD behavior, and grumbled about him while we waited in line for lunch.

Caught between wanting to be respected by the other teachers, and wanting to explain that Josh couldn't help what he was doing, I tried not to listen to the disgruntled talk, never mind joining the conversation as a way to bond with my coworkers. Instead, I scurried out of the line as fast as possible.

I felt as if I was betraying the other teachers by wanting to help this student. But should I betray the student instead?

All year, I watched as Josh struggled to maintain focus and concentration. At times, he would shine in his work, and at other times he would struggle. As we moved into the spring, and the first round of state tests began, I watched in agony as Josh struggled to sit through hours of testing. "Can't I get up now?" he'd plead with me. "Please?"

No matter how many detentions Josh served with me, I knew that the ADD would win. Josh always apologized and promised to do better the next day, and for a few days, he would do better, and then the restlessness, the speaking out of turn, and the inability to finish his work would all come back, and Josh would be back in detention.

Somewhere along the way, I learned that what Josh really needed was a place where he wasn't punished for something that raged out of his control.

When June arrived, I asked Josh to be my eighth-grade Teacher's Assistant (TA). The other teachers thought I was crazy.

Sometimes, I wondered.

But I also knew that TA Josh would be teaching me how to see beyond limitations, allowing me to find ways to provide a place where my students could be themselves.

That was a lesson I wanted to learn.

Classroom? What Classroom?

by T. Lloyd Reilly

I WORK AT a school attached to a boys' ranch. I spent two years as an assistant in the Student Alternative Center (SAC) before becoming a full-fledged teacher.

Our facility is part of a corporation that provides residential treatment for boys from the ages of seven to eighteen. Many of these children have been placed with us at the direction of the state Child Protective Services or the juvenile probation system. Many of our children suffer from some form of psychological disorder and behavior issues. This makes for an environment decidedly different from the typical school.

My first day as teacher, I showed up excited and ready for the new challenge. I was teaching computer technology, an area in which I had better-than-average knowledge, and I felt confident that I had everything under control.

Until I learned that my classroom was actually the former cafeteria. While I had nothing personal against cafeterias, they lacked the key ingredient necessary to serve the scheduled "meal" . . . computers.

How could I teach computer technology without any computers?

Before I had a chance to have that question answered, my students meandered into class. They looked at the cafeteria. They looked at me. They looked—in vain—for the computers.

They looked disgusted.

But wait! Here came a kindred soul! It was one of my regular students from the SAC room, who greeted me with a smile and a handshake and hug.

He said it was cool that I changed campuses, and asked me for a peanut butter and jelly sandwich (lunch menu for SAC).

The other kids snickered, and one asked me if I was a real teacher.

I sat down and began speaking about the computer system model. Having nothing to show them, I related the system model to the human gastrointestinal system. I told my students about the first computer being the size of a two-story building and only being capable of addition, subtraction, division, and multiplication. I told them that their brains were the most complex computers in the universe.

I taught them everything I could without actually having a computer in the room.

I glanced at the time.

"Did you know that taking a pee involves about a million times more computing power than the most complex video game?"

Once we actually got computers to work on, I became more of a traffic cop than computer teacher. Some of the students were already self-taught and exceeded my own skill level. They weren't interested in learning anything that couldn't be played, listened to, or down-loaded from a porn site when I wasn't looking.

These were not 1950s-sitcom kids.

When I wasn't chasing them off of MySpace, I could bribe them to practice their typing by offering free time to all who beat my typing speed. I slowed my pace, thinking to give them a fair chance. The first day, half the class got to play games for thirty minutes.

After that, I took the competition seriously, and so did my students. Everybody, myself included, eventually at least doubled their speed.

As my student from my SAC days told me, "Pretty freaking cool . . . this typing crap!" He started the year at eleven words per minute, and on the last day of school he pumped out seventy-five words per minute, without a mistake.

With these kids, I considered myself successful if they paid attention for more than twenty minutes in a class period. Many were Special Ed, and almost all had some kind of learning dysfunction.

Games were an outlet they used to push the world away, and when I barred my students from playing games the second semester, I received a measure of trouble. Once more I met the challenge, and attempted to get ahead of the curve by making my students design games using Microsoft PowerPoint and Paint.

The best times were when students gave me the Teacher's Ultimate Gift. You know, that look in their eyes that tells you the light bulb just went on. They understood . . . and thought it was cool.

I had less success with the staff. When I started, they greeted me with open arms, thinking they could stop teaching science. To that end, I tried to call the science teacher on the main campus to find out what I needed to do. My campus director thought I was calling to complain and jumped the gun by calling the superintendent, who then transferred science back to the other teachers, who assumed I'd double-crossed them.

I came to the teaching field rather late in life, becoming a first-year teacher in my mid-fifties, and I treat the end of year differently than do others on the staff.

I do not say goodbye. I hug my students, or shake their hands, and tell them to go softly.

These kids move around a lot. The state system dictates that you'll lose them before you really get to know them well, and then suddenly they'll be back.

I tell them I'll be here if they ever pass through again.

There's a garden to take care of here. Never can tell when it will blossom.

Taking Charge of the Cultural Classroom

by Dorit Sasson

ORIGINALLY FROM GREENWICH Village, Manhattan, I was a product of my environment.

Unfortunately, I began my first year in an elementary school located in Israel. My fourth-grade students were direct and verbal. I was introverted and reflective. I knew I had no choice but to act like an Israeli in order to survive in the cultural classroom.

I knew I needed to take control of this classroom before my students got the better of me.

As a new teacher, I had every single reason to worry. I was facing a classroom of twenty-four students who were more interested in each other than studying English.

I succeeded by creating a fun, non-threatening environment. I used songs, games, and an assortment of happy, sad, and mad faces to keep their attention and maintain discipline. Even with all of my efforts, however, I often felt I was doing little more than entertaining my students with my American accent.

They were forever restless.

During those the first few lessons, I taught Rosh Hashanah, the Jewish New Year, using a short song I wrote to the tune of "Heal the World," by Michael Jackson.

However, instead of playing the tape, I began the lesson by singing:

"Today is Thursday, tomorrow is Friday
Friday is the New Year
It is Rosh Hashanah
We eat apples and honey
It's a special day for you and for me."

After hearing me sing in my American accent, the students immediately broke into laughter. I couldn't continue. What had I been thinking, teaching about Rosh Hashanah by singing a Michael Jackson tune?

Holding the piece of chalk as if I wanted it to shatter, feeling the sweat dripping down my neck, I tried not to react in any way that would show my disappointment.

Telling the students we were now going to focus on the vocabulary part of the lesson, I wrote on the board:

1. apples
2. honey
3. special
4. day
5. you
6. me

7. Thursday
8. Friday

In Hebrew, I told them to go to sleep so I could erase a word, which I would then have them guess. While I'd meant for them to close their eyes, and hoped for quiet, they laughed and made snoring noises.

When I later showed them a picture of the letter "A" (Aa), they jumped out of their seats as if I'd left the room.

I got the impression I was not reaching my goal of playing the tough Israeli teacher. As my students ran wild, days of sweat were followed by nights of tears. I had to do something differently.

During my free time, I began to observe the behavior of the other teachers so that I could imitate them.

I began using Hebrew to control my students, the language with which they were disciplined by their parents.

I even hung a whistle around my neck.

These were not part of my teaching and management style, but I realized I would have to learn a whole new way of running a classroom if I was going to teach these students English.

I heard my mentor's voice saying, "Don't start a lesson until you have absolute complete quiet." In the beginning, I had waited at least ten minutes. Now I called for silence in Hebrew, despite the fact that my didactic counselor had strongly advised speaking to the students in anything but English.

She wasn't standing here in front of this class. I was.

I implemented a classroom point system to encourage good behavior. I awarded prizes. Over a period of weeks and months, more students listened and learned. As we came closer to sticking to my plan, I slept more and worried less.

Four months after the school year began, I brought in a rather big blackboard marked into nine squares. Above the top three squares were labels for A-B-C, and to the left of the side squares were labels for 1-2-3.

My students straightened.

"What's that?" asked one boy.

"You'll see," I replied.

I turned the board away from them and filled the squares before explaining how this was going to work.

They had to guess the word I was thinking of from a word bank written on the board. They would guess by giving me the number and letter of the word's position. If they guessed the word correctly based on the clues I gave, they received a point for their team.

I showed them the words on the board.

They became so absorbed by the concept of winning that they did not realize they were learning. They enjoyed the guessing-game format and the smiley faces they received. They were engaged.

After that lesson, I lugged my game upstairs and through the ruby hallways. I arrived in the teacher's room thinking, "What a lesson!"

While I wanted to share my success, the teachers were all either sipping coffee or deep in conversation. Finally, I found my mentor, who was a general education teacher, sitting in a corner with another of the English teachers.

The two of them were talking about the upcoming English Day, which included special activities and games around the subject of learning English. The timing couldn't have been better. I described how well my activity went. "They jumped out of their seats to answer," I said excitedly.

"That's great!" my mentor said. "You can demonstrate on English Day."

And so I did, presenting each student with a certificate. One Ethiopian student flashed me a wide smile I will never forget.

I'm not sure I ever emulated my Israeli counterparts. What I did, in the final outcome, was take bits of the Israeli personality, bits of my Greenwich Village personality, and bits of my teacher personality to create a workable solution to the cultural classroom.

L'Chayim.

Here's to Bad Teaching Days

by Camille Subramaniam

EVERY PERSON HAS bad hair days. Every teacher has bad teaching days.

When you're experiencing a bad teaching day, you must try to ignore the image of a poised veteran teacher standing at the chalkboard with the perfect shining apple on the corner of the desk. Know that tomorrow is another day, a day that will be just a bit easier because of what you're learning today.

There are three lifelines that helped me get through my first year of bad teaching days:

- It's not like someone's going to die if . . .
- They're gonna learn something
- Revision is your friend

I can't claim credit for the first lifeline. It was passed down to me during my days as a reporter, but applies even more so to the rigors of teaching. On one really bad reporting day, I was struggling to get my story on the air. My news director patiently—yet quickly—finished editing my work when I felt like giving up.

Afterward, he told me, "You have to keep it in perspective, Camille. It's not like someone's going to die if we don't get your story on the air."

With the exception of medical professionals and cage fighters, I think most people can apply the words, "It's not like someone's going to die if . . ."

Even on my worst day as a teacher, none of my students died as a direct result of my teaching methods.

Sure, there have been days . . . But we're going to assume that none of your students have dropped into a pit of flaming lava, and move on to lifeline number two.

"They're gonna learn something."

Let me share one of my first teaching failures with you.

After reading multiple versions of "Little Red Riding Hood" from around the world, the students were asked to write an essay comparing themselves to one of the characters in the story. Okay, so maybe it was a weird assignment, but it seemed like a good idea at the time.

Most students misread the prompt (probably because it's a weird one) and inserted themselves into the story.

I expected to get a bunch of analytical essays. What I got back was fairy tale turned sci-fi horror flick. I read about students running in with axes over their shoulders to save Red and Grandmother. I read about sly, manipulative students cross-dressing in Granny's clothes. I read about students dressed in red capes traipsing through the forest picking flowers.

The students hated the assignment. I hated reading their papers.

Here's to Bad Teaching Days

What did I learn from this ill-fated essay?

They're gonna learn something. Within the framework of Little Red Riding Hood, the students learned something about who they were, or who they wished they were, or how they thought they were perceived.

After I explained that I'd been less than clear when describing the assignment, I asked them to modify their initial drafts.

The students then came up with creative ways to identify themselves with the characters they'd portrayed.

Some students saw themselves in the ambitious and resourceful wolf. Some identified with Red's innocence, and others with the woodcutter's courage.

While initially I'd been shocked at how the original assignment had been interpreted, I would say in the end that the students not only learned about the importance of revision, but also learned more about themselves than they would have if I'd been able to explain what I'd wanted the first time.

Students will learn something in your class because they have an uncanny way of taking a task, thinking creatively and critically, and solving problems in an interesting and fresh way. Even if your teaching isn't flawless on day one—or day one thousand—know that your students will come prepared to use what you give them, do their job, and learn.

You will learn something, too, as a student of your own teaching. I'm happy to say my writing prompts have improved as a result of embracing my third lifeline: Revision is my friend.

The derivation of the word "revision" literally means "seeing again." After a bad teaching day, actually replay the day in your mind's eye. Look at what worked and what didn't work. Envision changes you can implement that will lead to a good teaching day next time.

There will always be a next time. A next semester. A new set of students.

By the end of my first year in the classroom, I had used these three lifelines to develop an assignment that remains, to this day, a student favorite. The essay has students evaluate their own learning process.

First, students must interact with members of a group they would not normally associate with. Then, they spend time with the group. At the end of the project, students describe the re-vision of their ideas by comparing their point of view before, during, and after learning about the organization.

Erica, a student with a fear of heights, decided to investigate a local rock-climbing club. Erica assumed that the club's members consisted of adrenaline-junky, extreme-sport, and Evel Knievel types. As a result of talking with a few of the members, she learned that many join to overcome their fear of heights.

Isn't this the same process we undergo as beginning teachers? We go into teaching with preconceived notions and guesses about what it means to be a great teacher. Then we sift through the words of experienced teachers and make our own first attempts in order to produce a new vision of our teaching.

Our new vision is in turn smashed to bits by bad days, which allows us to revise our theories, preparing us for the next bad day, when we repeat the process, accumulating experience and the confidence to persevere.

Here's to bad teaching days. They make for better teachers.

As to bad hair days, well, they're just bad.

Blue Hawaii

by Terri Elders

SINCE SOME OF my students were only eight years my junior when I started teaching in 1963, I valued the warnings of seasoned teachers about the need to preserve professional distance. Sometimes, all that distinguished me from the kids were my high heels and nylons.

With my sophomore journalism and English classes, I easily maintained a decorous distance. I lectured that hands would be raised, assignments would be followed, and English would be spoken. When students forgot, and let slip a slang "dude" or "going ape," I rephrased the comment before reminding them that English was the official language in my classroom.

Advanced Journalism was a different story.

Maybe the problem stemmed from the class being located next to the campus lunch area, or maybe it stemmed from my working so closely with the students on tight deadlines, but a line was crossed.

We were lunchtime scribes, throwing together a killer edition of the school newspaper, with a sidebar of surf-focused conversation. Although my veteran hot-doggers insisted they could smell the saltier air when the tide came in fifteen miles south, and the extent of my beach expertise consisted of knowing when to layer on my sunscreen lotion, it was difficult not to join in on the jabber.

My students listened to the Beach Boys more than the Beatles, and their bleached locks stood out among the popular new mop-tops. They lugged around copies of James Michener's *Hawaii* and studied by lava lamp. The girls sported puka shell jewelry, and the boys urged them to trade their minis for hula skirts.

Even the Snack Shack, where my Advanced Journalism students grabbed something to eat before returning to edit page proofs, appeared to fall prey to the craze when they tacked up woven grass wall-coverings and a bamboo-framed panoramic Polynesian mural.

While the Shack was only promoting the introduction of a new confection, Hawaiian Ice, my students reacted as if the kiosk had been transformed into an outpost of Don the Beachcomber's, and as if our Room 355 was located on the shores of Waikiki.

Their speech cadences grew melodic, with murmurs of *mahalo* and *aloha*. Some even tried to call me the Big Kahuna, which I put a stop to immediately.

After all, I was trying to maintain professional distance.

When they offered to bring me back an Ice from the Shack, I politely declined and munched apple slices instead. I reminded myself never to pack pineapple slices, for fear my students would be convinced I'd gone native.

During my first-period English class, students called my attention to a minor classroom change. "Look, Teach," they chorused, "doesn't the bookcase look bitchin'?"

I wheeled around and stared at an explosion of artificial leis draped in rainbow hues on the cabinet's knobs. Then I noticed similar embellishments on all the window cranks.

As I turned back to face my students, I assumed my mature schoolmarm tone. "First, it's Mrs. Elders, not 'Teach,' and second, I thought we agreed we wouldn't say that word in this class. This is English."

The tenth graders nodded solemnly. Some muttered, "Sorry." I thought I heard somebody whisper, "Holy Pele!"

Had I been too harsh? No. Even though I knew that "bitchin'," a popular slang expression, simply meant "awesome," it set teeth on edge. And none of the teachers allowed students to address them by nicknames.

"Who put up the leis?" I asked, hoping to maintain common ground. Twenty-five heads shook back and forth like metronomes.

Come fourth period, the Advanced Journalism class also feigned innocence. "Don't know where the leis came from," they said, "but it's beginning to look like surf's up."

A few mornings later I found a potted anthurium with large, waxy, scarlet petals by the side of the bookcase, and a rattan basket full of silk dendrobium orchids on my desk. Mischief this might be, I decided, but it certainly brightened up the old room.

"Just so long as they don't show up sipping Mai Tais and Zombies," I reassured myself. The decorations weren't vandalism, and no one was being hurt.

Later, during fourth period, a few of my students announced they were going to the Shack for some Ice before putting the newspaper to bed. "Don't you want to try some?"

Sighing, I fished for some change. "Bring me something delicious."

What they brought me was a paper cone cup filled with the creamiest, fruitiest, most delectable blue raspberry treat I'd ever tasted, and I savored every tangy lick, sip, and slurp.

In fact, that Ice seemed to fuel the rest of my day. Even the students in my sixth-period class seemed particularly attentive, never taking their eyes from my face. Was it what I was saying, reviewing the possible topics for their presentations? Or was it how I felt, as though I stood on an endless beach, buffeted by warm ocean breezes?

At the final bell, I learned the truth.

As the students filed from the room, one stopped by my desk and held out her compact. "You might want to take a look."

I glanced at the mirror and then stared in horror at my blue lips. My blue tongue. Even my teeth glowed with an appalling blueness.

And that was the end of letting my professionalism slip.

While the school newspaper went on to win a local award that year, and several of my students qualified for Quill and Scroll, the National High School Journalism Society, I learned that teaching was a balancing act—not unlike surfboarding—and sometimes you wiped out.

My second year, Hawaii gave way to Liverpool, but I refused to admit which of the Fab Four was my fave rave. After all, a young teacher had to maintain professional distance.

Blue Hawaii

Pizza

by Emily Warren

MY FIRST YEAR in the classroom consisted of days that all started the same.

The shiny glob of keys jingle-jangled from my neck, sweat pouring from places I didn't know had glands, as I raced with that dreaded stack of thirty ripping folders crammed with crumpled paper. At least ten of the folders were supposed to have been dropped in a different class's bin, five were missing, and one finally exploded to become a yellow brick road for sneaker prints.

Voices called in bad harmony that sounded like beautiful a cappella as I entered the room. "Hi, Miss Warren!" *"Hola, flaca!"* "What's good, Miss Warren G Funk?"

Then came the unanswerable questions.

The unanswerable questions were the only thing that remained certain to me during my crazy first days as an eleventh-grade English teacher.

No matter how many hours I spent Googling images to put on worksheets the night before. No matter how many hours I spent printing copies of yesterday's handouts for the students saying, "I can't find" and "you never gave me" and "I wasn't ever here!" No matter how many hours I spent grading quizzes with red scribbles and stick figures and stickers and "hahaha"s. No matter how many hours I prepared and prepped, I would always get at least ten unanswerable questions when I entered the classroom.

The questions were flung at me within three minutes after the first bell rang, while I stumbled around trying to balance and hold back the avalanche of torn folders weighing twice what I did on a bloated day:

- Did you grade my notebook?
- Can I sit next to Kate if we promise not to talk?
- What's that on your chin?
- Are we going to do something fun today?
- Can I e-mail you my paper tonight, or will you still take ten points off?
- Can I go get a Band-Aid?
- Do you have extra copies of the *Macbeth* paper?
- What did I miss when I was absent last Thursday?
- Why's school so stupid?
- What did I get on my quiz?
- Why isn't my notebook in the bin?
- Can you come tell me if I did my homework right? I wrote from the point of view of a toilet!

The unanswerable questions came in bursts. The unanswerable questions came all at once.

If I ever thought I was one person, one woman, one friend, or one lover, that notion disappeared as soon as I staggered into the classroom, where my students turned me into a pizza pie cut into sixty pieces, cheese hanging from slice to slice, sauce dripping all over the place.

As soon as I entered my classroom, I was no longer a whole person, a plain pie that shared the same ladle of sauce and cup of grated mozzarella.

Instead, I was a mushroom slice for Amanda, who said she couldn't be creative. I was a three-veggie for Lysette, whose button popped off of her favorite jeans. I was a bacon and pineapple (sprinkled with ephedrine) for Tyrell, who actually tried to keep his eyes open but couldn't. I was a plain, original, practical slice for Tiffany, whose mother kicked the crap out of her one night and then hugged and loved her the next morning. I was two slices with extra cheese for Roberto, who waited outside for his father, who never showed up, and Roberto told me through tears that he hadn't seen in more than two years.

The students didn't sit quietly and wait for their slice to be delivered. They were starved and they would rush me, grabbing with both hands. They gorged themselves and purged if necessary.

Students have their backsides leaned up against the metal chairs at different angles, some sweating, some cold, some fast asleep with pins and needles. Students' pulses beat at different paces.

As the teacher, I am the education, the friend, the disciplinarian, the nemesis, the big-time crush, the laughingstock of every single one of them. Most pizza places won't make a pie with more variety than half and half. I tried once to order a pie with two pepperoni slices, one red pepper, one anchovy, one sausage, and three plain. The man on the other end hung up on me.

I think I understand why.

RT (1982)

by Kathleen A. Montgomery

PEOPLE ARE QUICK to say that children can be cruel, and rattle off any number of schoolyard experiences.

When I became a teacher, I rememberd the opposite was also true: Children could be more open than most adults, and sometimes they could say what needed to be said.

"Why is Robbie wearing his hat in class?"

I froze for just a second before plastering a smile on my face. Of course I'd been a fool to think none of the other first graders would notice the woolen cap, but hadn't wanted to change today's planned discussion from early explorers to chemotherapy.

"I've spoken to Robbie's parents, and he has permission to wear his hat in class," I said. The hat was a woolen winter cap, especially out of place during these still-warm days of late September.

Just as I'd been taught by my own professors, I had handled the situation. Now it was back to teaching.

Seven-year-old Jessica raised her hand and squirmed in her seat, which wasn't in any way unusual for the little ball of fire.

"Jessica?"

"Miss Montgomery, won't Robbie's head get hot?"

"If that happens, I'm sure that Robbie knows what to do." While I didn't like talking about Robbie in the third person, I wanted to deflect the attention away from him before returning to the early explorers.

Mark raised his hand.

"Mark?"

"Can I wear my hat in class?"

I shouldn't have been surprised, since Mark was always quick to jump on any bandwagon, especially if it was rolling downhill toward a cliff.

"That would be something I would need to discuss with your parents. That answer goes for everybody else. Robbie is currently the only person who has permission to wear a hat in class. Understand?"

As my students reluctantly nodded, I moved toward the blackboard, signaling an end to that particular discussion.

"Miss Montgomery?"

I turned around and said, "Yes?"

Valerie gushed with helpfulness, "Maybe Robbie should change his seat so he's closer to the window. That way his head won't get so hot."

My anxiety began to build. Things like this had never happened in methods class. Of course no one had ever thrown up all over my brand-new shoes there, as they had here on my very first day, all over my brand-new shoes.

I forced myself to become calm.

RT (1982)

"Robbie, would you like to change seats?"

He shook his head. His parents told me that Robbie was bearing up well under the pressure, that he didn't want to be treated differently from any other first grader.

I informed my students that Robbie was happy in his present seat. I used my teacher voice, my no-nonsense voice. The subject was closed.

Becka raised her hand, a rare event for a child sorely lacking in confidence.

"Becka, do you have a question about early explorers?"

"Yes, Miss Montgomery."

"Go ahead then." I'd scored high in classroom management.

"If Robbie—"

I interrupted, "I thought you had a question about early explorers."

Becka nodded vigorously, and said, "I do. If Robbie was on the ship with Christopher Columbus, would he still want to wear his hat?"

My first week, a veteran teacher had told me that every class was different, and I never needed to fear falling into a rut because each batch of children brought new challenges. A rut? It was my first week!

While I didn't know whether this challenge made this class unique, I knew that this group of children would never drop a topic until they felt every single possible question had been asked and answered.

"Robbie," I paused long enough for him to find reassurance in my smile. "If you were on the ship with Christopher Columbus, do you think you'd still want to wear your hat?"

"Yes, Miss Montgomery," he paused. "I'll always want to wear my hat."

"Thank you. Now, back to the early explorers."

Several students asked Robbie why.

My breath caught in my throat. Would he answer? If so, how? Should I interrupt and take control? When I tried, I found I couldn't speak.

Robbie looked at the top of his desk and said, "Because I look funny."

There it was, out in the open, the fear of being ridiculed by his classmates. If anybody knew children could be cruel, it was other children. I don't know who was more afraid at that moment, Robbie or me.

Valerie waved her hand. "Miss Montgomery?"

"Yes, Valerie."

"Can I just say one thing?"

I took a deep breath. "Of course."

Better to get it over with now. Anything they didn't say in class, they'd sing on the playground, or whisper in the hall. At least here I could try to control the situation and minimize the damage.

Valerie turned to her classmate. "Robbie, you don't have to wear a winter hat. ET looks funny, and we love him."

As Robbie slid the woolen cap from his head, I pulled out my chair and sat before my knees let go.

Sometimes it takes a child.

Reading the Riot Act

by Monica Whitaker

THIS READING GROUP again. Crazy again. Fourth graders running in the four square feet of open floor space, running at the mouth.

They were supposed to be the high-level readers, the ones capable of enriched literary study. But my glower, my best command voice, and my angel-of-death, head-to-toe black outfits hadn't fazed this crew as it had my obedient, regular class. Literary circles can't begin with anarchy.

At least, not these kind of literary circles.

When I'd allowed this reading group to take bathroom breaks, they'd formed a steady march to the toilet stalls like ants that hit jackpot on a jelly doughnut. When allowed to whisper, the students spoke. If allowed to speak, they yelled. When permitted to sharpen pencils, they broke the tips for an excuse to get up.

"They're taking advantage of you," their homeroom teacher frowned.

Following up on that ever-so-helpful frown, I decided to make some changes.

I'd given them an inch and they'd taken a mile. That meant it was time to take that inch back.

Today marked the crackdown.

I laid it out straight, just as soon as they took their seats.

"In the past two weeks, this group has been brazen, inconsiderate, and disrespectful," I told them. "This classroom operates on four requirements: personal responsibility; respect for others; respect for the environment; and constant striving for excellence. I'm seeing little of it."

Their faces looked up at me. Were they listening? Were they comprehending? Were they even awake?

"So," I continued, "as of today, we have new classroom policies and procedures."

I was eliminating bathroom breaks except for emergencies. "It's an hour-and-a-half stretch," I said. "You can hold it."

Gone, too, was the ability to get out of seats without permission.

Got to throw something away? Raise your hand.

Broken pencil? Raise your hand.

Need a Kleenex? Raise your hand.

Any questions? No? Good.

So began my experiment in containment. Day one, first week of October.

I started the lesson.

We had gone through the vocabulary introduction and summarized what happened in our novel's last chapter when the class started testing the new boundaries. When James, cheeks puffed, held his left hand aloft and wriggled his fingers to get my attention, he gave me the opportunity to prove I meant business.

"Do you need a tissue?" I asked.

He shook his head.

"Are you sick?"

No response. Not a shake, nothing.

"Forget it," I said, turning back to my notes. "You're not playing that game in here."

I should have reined in this reading group from the very beginning. Set definite guidelines, make sure they're followed, and the classroom runs like a well-oiled machine.

"Mmm," James said, and then he vomited on my floor.

While the custodian was quick to answer my 9-1-1 cleanup plea, the smell of cat litter only seemed to intensify the stench of vomit. The compounded aroma was so distracting that even I had trouble remembering the author's purpose.

Then Pauline entered the room, late due to her visit to the school counselor, and interrupted the discussions with a loud greeting. She twitched her shoulders and jangled both arms, clearly in full meltdown mode. She huffed as I sent her out for a second try at entering the room correctly.

Must maintain discipline.

"Her meds haven't kicked in yet," the counselor whispered.

I'd just found my place in the book when Kayla's tooth fell out.

David chattered rather than simply stating an answer.

Pauline slammed her books repeatedly on the desk. While I moved Pauline to her time-out seat, Alexia, hand still in the air, got up to help herself to a tissue. I looked up sharply.

"What were my instructions regarding getting out of your seat?" I demanded.

"You said to raise your hand, but . . ."

Alexia pulled her other hand away from her nose, exposing an inch-long trail of mucus. Her classmates recoiled in horror.

At least I didn't need to call the janitor again.

The rest of the time passed quickly. Somehow, miraculously, the reading group focused enough to read the next chapter, discuss the purpose for this selection, and answer questions that required them to infer something about the characters.

Maybe before the students could follow the new procedures, they just need to get things out of their system, things like vomit, teeth, and mucus.

After the hour and a half was up, the reading group formed a line without talking. They'd never before left my room without having to go back and try it again.

Of course, the lingering scent of vomit may have contributed to their obedience.

But I felt like going to that homeroom teacher and nonchalantly describing how well reading group had gone today, because of my classroom management skills. Of course, if I left out the vomit, the tooth, and the mucus, it wasn't really much of a story.

Quiet Time in the Fourth Grade

by Ed Dwyer

AFTER GRADUATING FROM college, I spent the next two years in the Army. I then returned home and accepted a fourth-grade teaching position at a school located in the center of a small city.

Things started off fairly well, but the small room soon reverberated with the sounds of hectic disorder and misbehavior. Counting me, there were thirty-four people in that space, which meant thirty-four egos and thirty-four attitudes.

As situations arose, I found myself constantly reacting, which left me feeling overwhelmed. Especially when several situations arose at once.

Being new to the school, I didn't want anyone to know how I was feeling, to know my doubts and difficulties. Showing weakness didn't seem the wisest of moves at this point in my fledgling career.

Perhaps this classroom, a collection of children with behavior problems culled from several feeder schools, was this school administration's version of basic training: put me in front of the worst possible classroom to see if I could be broken.

Perhaps the opposite was true. Perhaps I should consider this classroom a compliment to my perceived teaching skills. Or recognition that I was just out of the military and thus an expert concerning discipline.

The fall moved on to winter and any change was not for the better. I struggled daily but managed to survive. However, I was not thriving. I was not enjoying teaching.

I thought about taking a class at the university but I didn't want to listen to lectures on "curriculum development" and "philosophy of education." I didn't need theory. I needed practical solutions.

Then, while reading a newspaper one evening, I saw a listing of classes offered at the continuing education center in a nearby city. Among the classes listed was a brief description of a class in yoga.

Well, I certainly hadn't tried yoga as a discipline technique. What could it hurt to try?

I thought the matter over and then enrolled.

The instructor had been born in India and had studied yoga and meditation in Tibet. The yoga classes were invigorating and moved rhythmically from one activity to another, except for a pause occurring around the middle of the one-hour session.

During this pause the teacher appeared to just sit and do nothing while the group sat watching.

Finally, after several sessions, someone in the group politely asked, "Why do you stop class and just sit there quietly for five minutes?"

The teacher paused a moment and replied, "I am praying. I am praying for you. One by one, I take each of you into my heart and I think about you. I wish good things for you. Then I release you from my heart, take into my heart the next person, and do the same thing. This is a very important part of my class."

I was impressed by his sincerity, by how warm his efforts made me feel toward him, and by how good they made me feel about myself.

I thought about that answer for several days. The teacher's words stayed with me, and I decided to follow his example with my own students.

Perhaps the key to managing my students was not disciplining them, but increasing my own self-discipline.

In the usual midmorning bustle of class the next day, I very calmly told the children: "I need a few minutes to think about you. I'll sit at my desk and think about each of you. This will be my quiet time. Please work quietly and please don't come to see me or raise your hand unless it's very important."

Somewhat to my surprise, the students seemed to consider my request reasonable and were more cooperative than usual, working quietly and independently for those five minutes.

I did as the yoga teacher explained. I thought about each child individually. Each child in turn became the focus of my attention. Things I thought I would remember but had either overlooked or forgotten suddenly came back to me.

For example, I remembered how Michael looked when he told me the day before, "My dog died last night. He got hit by a car."

I remembered how fearful Debbie was, thinking she would be punished when she got home because she broke the clasp on her necklace.

Most of all, the quiet children came to mind.

After all, there were some well-behaved children in my classroom. Unfortunately, they tended to disappear in all the background noise.

The one class became thirty-three individual children, all of whom had good times, hard times, and times in between these two extremes.

For some reason, this made dealing with them easier. Instead of a flailing mob, they became separate people who could be helped and taught.

Quiet time became a regular and highly valued part of my school day. Sometimes I took brief notes during the quiet time to serve as reminders. My whole outlook changed.

Instead of frantically, emotionally, and globally reacting to situations, I focused on the accomplishments of individual children and on issues that needed to be resolved. I discovered that my own growing sense of calmness affected the children as if by osmosis because they seemed calmer too.

I can't recommend quiet time enough.

This time not only does engaging in quiet time link a personal appreciation for each child with instruction, classroom management, and academics, it also provides an opportunity for simple reflection.

How much do we miss because we just go, go, go?

In this age of high-stakes testing and demands for accountability, a moment to reflect can slow the pace down, increasing enjoyment and productivity.

Better still, such reflection has demonstrated to me that some of the most effective classroom time occurred when the least effort was being expended!

Substitute Initiation

by Tina Haapala

WHEN I WAS LAID off from my regular job due to budget cuts, I seized the opportunity to escape the cubicle life, at least for a while.

It was February, and flu season was in full swing. With so many teacher absences, the local schools needed as many substitute teachers as they could find.

After a quick orientation, I was ready to go, and off I went.

The sixth-grade history teacher I was replacing warned me that it might be a difficult day because the students were not going to be able to go to their PE class or recess. Most of the other students were taking the state assessment tests, so the school had to stay very quiet.

When my students returned from lunch, something had changed. Their usual chattering was sprinkled with muffled giggles. I tried to pinpoint the source in order to learn the cause, but the students had mastered being "sly."

"Ms. H? Can you help me with this?"

I crossed to the far side of the room and asked "With what?"

The student seemed to pick a passage at random, and when I read it aloud, he didn't pay the least amount of attention. Meanwhile, the giggles continued.

"Did that help?"

"Yes. Thanks."

I returned to my desk. I reminded myself that these were sixth graders, the oldest kids in this elementary school. They'd certainly experienced enough substitute teachers not to giggle just because there was a stranger behind their teacher's desk.

Something was up.

A student on the other side of the room asked me for help.

As soon as I reached his desk, the whole class busted out in laughter.

"Okay, what's so funny?" I didn't want to come down too hard because I was still skeptical of my first-year instincts. I didn't have any proof these students were trying to get away with anything.

One of them tried to soothe me. "Something funny happened at lunch, and now we have the giggles."

Fine. I tried to remain upbeat, to be grateful the students were happy rather than miserable, but I kept my eyes and ears open. Too many of them were smothering giggles and smiles.

A few minutes later, a student asked if I liked the color red.

That's when I smelled the ketchup.

I answered the question and tried to act like nothing had changed.

At least I had some idea what was going on. The air seemed thick with tomato. How could I have missed it before now?

I looked in the desk drawers. Left. Right. Middle.

Substitute Initiation

I looked in my purse. I was more than relieved that no one had been in it.

I stood up and walked around the room.

The smell seemed to be everywhere.

When I returned to my desk, I saw an empty ketchup packet next to the black chair I'd been sitting in. I touched the seat. My fingertip was a nice, watery red.

Well, that explained why the smell was following me.

The room had gone quiet.

I said nothing as I grabbed a few tissues and wiped off the teacher's chair, and then made a half-hearted attempt at my own pants. I was never so happy to have chosen black slacks that morning.

How did I handle this? Going for the principal meant leaving the students alone when the rest of the school was busy taking tests. I also wasn't thrilled with the idea of admitting my incompetence.

I walked to the middle of the classroom. "Who did that?"

Of course there was no response.

"Well," I said, "I have ketchup on the seat of my pants. A lot of it. Hopefully, it will come out. While I don't know for sure who was responsible, I want to let you all know that this was my first time at your school. This is what I'm going to remember about you and your school. You are halfway thorough sixth grade. You are supposed to be the most mature of all the students in the building. I'm very disappointed."

I was careful not to raise my voice. "The joke is over. It's done. We will now return our focus to the reason we're here."

Although initially stunned into silence by my subdued lecture, the students were loud and hectic the rest of the afternoon. After they left, I wrote a detailed note for the teacher, telling her what had occurred, describing my initiation as a substitute teacher.

A few days later, I received an e-mail from the principal. He apologized for how the students had acted, and related the punishments he'd given them.

A few days after that, I received letters of apology from most of the students. Between the phrases probably borrowed from the lecture they'd been given, I could hear their true voices.

Some of them rationalized their behavior: "I didn't want my friends to hate me if I warned you about the ketchup." "I didn't want to get my friends in trouble." Some of them empathized: "If I was a sub I wouldn't want ketchup on my pants."

The ketchup came out of my black pants easily, and in the end, only my dignity was hurt.

While I didn't like having left the task of disciplining to others, I realized that sometimes there is no substitute for the regular teacher. Nothing I could have said or done would have been as effective as the students being disciplined by the person they saw at the front of the classroom every day.

I also recognized that most students, especially those on the verge of teen-hood, were hardwired to test boundaries. "We've got a sub! How far can we go?"

Well, they'd tested the boundaries and tasted the consequences. They'd learned something valuable that wasn't on that day's lesson plan.

I'd learned something as well.

There's no substitute for your basic black.

Mary

by Teresa Ives Lilly

THE PRINCIPAL STOOD in the doorway of my special education class and took a deep breath before she announced, "You have a new student."

I looked around at my full room. This class was the drop-off for any students the other teachers found too difficult.

"Who is it?" I asked, feeling less than enthusiastic. My first year of teaching was an incredible challenge, every single day, and I was ill prepared to take on more.

"Her name is Mary." The principal pushed a small girl into the room, handed me her file, and left. No visitor ever stayed in my classroom very long.

Mary was a frightened eight-year-old Hispanic girl, with dirty, stringy hair that hung straight to her shoulders. She had black eyes and a glorious smile. Mary was a child who would not speak, except that from time to time she would utter vulgar words. Mary was a child who had failed first grade, and no one had noticed that she did not know the letters of the alphabet.

Mary was an innocent girl who had been molested at home by her mother's boyfriend, but no one knew about it until they found her sitting in a small pool of blood on her chair in school.

This was the new addition to my already full class. Mary, the child who stole my heart that very first day.

"Hello, Mary. My name is Miss Lilly."

At first, I allowed Mary to just wander around the room. She did not trust me. She watched as I worked with other students. However, it did not take long before she was willing to participate. She wanted to enjoy the treats and earn the prizes that I gave for good work. She quickly began working in the folder I had set up for her.

As the year progressed, Mary began to come to me for hugs. Mary did her schoolwork, but she did not speak. The only exception was the time I heard her tell a dirty story to the other children about what was under her dress.

Mary had been placed with a foster family. She seemed to be doing well there. Her mother had been diagnosed as mentally retarded, and the boyfriend had been declared an illegal immigrant and deported to Mexico. A grandparent program was set up to help Mary's mother make better decisions. Of course, all these things took time.

Over that time, Mary blossomed into a beautiful flower.

When there were only two months left of school, I decided our class would present a play to the whole school. The children were so excited they would have ignored their regular schoolwork if I let them. They wanted to practice all the time.

Even Mary wanted to be in the play. She was going to represent a star in the song "Do You Hear What I Hear?" She was also going to dance with a group of children to the song "A Spoon Full of Sugar."

Mary never spoke her line during practice. She just smiled, laughed at me, and ran around when it was her turn.

The play was going to be a fiasco. I just knew it. Still, I felt the students needed a chance to have their shining moment, so we pushed on.

Despite her performance in first grade, Mary turned out to be smart. She was advancing in her academics at a surprising rate, and there was talk about putting her back into a regular classroom next year.

Although I would miss her, I would not consider holding her back.

Meanwhile, after months of practice, the day of the play finally arrived. Costumes were on, the students in place. Mary was all smiles. My heart was singing.

The curtain was pulled and the play began.

Prepared for the worst, I was pleasantly surprised at how well the children were doing.

Mary's line was coming up. I was ready to say her line for her, but at just the right moment, Mary's voice rang out clear as a bell.

The teachers and principal applauded.

The other students stopped the whole play in order to announce to me that Mary had spoken. I encouraged them to continue, and they did. The show ended with the dance. Mary performed perfectly.

I couldn't imagine being prouder of the accomplishments of my own children.

After the play, the principal stopped in my room.

"Mary won't be coming back to school tomorrow," she told me. "Mary is returning to live with her mother, and they no longer live in this school district."

Although my heart was heavy, Mary seemed happy about the idea of moving back with her mother. She talked to me many times about the exciting news. Mary was the star of the day.

The next time I saw Mary, it was not with smiles and laughter. Two weeks after she left my classroom, Mary returned with her mother and the grandparent team to collect her books.

Mary did not run up to me and hug me. She did not take any notice of her classmates. She did not smile and she did talk.

Mary did not speak at all. My visitor that day was the frightened, eight-year-old girl with dirty shoulder-length hair. Mary stayed huddled away from us all.

There was no laughter. There were no words.

I still pray for her every day.

Beautiful

by Kelly Wilson

BUS DUTY. AGAIN.

I dodged crowds of kids filling the hallway, chattering and laughing, looking everywhere but where they were going. Still, they managed to get there, if not quickly enough for my taste.

"Come on, guys, you're gonna miss the bus," I nagged, the obligatory mantra at the end of each school day.

Surrounded by students heading home, I wondered whether I was in the right career. The job was more than I had expected—more difficult, more stressful, more draining.

As I reviewed the events of the day, I wondered whether I'd scarred anybody for life. Had I made the right decisions? Had I smiled enough? Had I smiled at all?

As I herded the kids through the school doors, I wondered if I was really meant to be a teacher.

"Buses are late again," Rachel Morgan said as I finally arrived outside, the kids fidgeting in lines arranged by color: red, blue, green, and orange. "If you're all set, I'll go back in."

"Thanks, Mrs. Morgan." I rolled my eyes. "Who else has bus duty?"

"Dave."

"Good." Dave Hamilton, Rachel, and I were starting our teaching careers at the same time. "He has more energy than some of the more 'experienced' teachers. In fact—"

I nodded to a couple of second-grade teachers who had their backs to the kids as they chatted with the principal.

Chuckling, Rachel went inside.

Since the kids were keeping themselves entertained, I took a moment for myself, filling my lungs with the fresh air of late spring as the sun warmed my face.

The sound of students wrestling on the grass brought me back to reality, and I split them up. "Let's watch for the buses."

I caught a glimpse of yellow salvation at the intersection, only to watch it turn the opposite direction.

Dave held his arms in the air. "All right, you guys, time to play 'Mr. Hamilton says!'"

The students turned toward him expectantly.

"Mr. Hamilton says, hop on one foot!"

Heads bobbed as kids obeyed.

What a great idea, I thought.

"Mr. Hamilton says, hop on the other foot!"

Kids switched feet, arms out to keep balance.

"Stop hopping!"

Most still bobbed while a third of the group stopped. They groaned at his announcement: "YOU'RE OUT! I didn't say 'Mr. Hamilton says!'"

Some of those who weren't "out" clapped in delight.

"Okay, everybody, Mr. Hamilton says, stick out your tongue!"

"What if I'm out?"

"Everybody plays."

I focused on the road, looking for any sign of dirty yellow, longing to smell the diesel fumes of freedom.

"Mr. Hamilton says, reach for the stars!"

Why couldn't the buses ever get here on time?

"Mr. Hamilton says, yell 'Mrs. Wilson is beautiful!'"

Had I heard correctly? My question was answered by chorus of kids yelling, "Mrs. Wilson is beautiful!"

I looked at the two other second-grade teachers and the principal, who were paying no attention to the game.

"Not loud enough! Mr. Hamilton says, yell 'Mrs. Wilson is beautiful!'"

My mind whirled as I flipped through my options: blushing, protesting, laughing. I decided to play along, smiling and vamping for the students.

Where were those buses?

A few "Mr. Hamilton says" later, the buses finally ground to a halt in front of the kids.

I avoided looking Dave in the eyes as I got the students loaded and then rushed back inside.

Cornering Rachel in her classroom, I took a deep breath before shutting the door.

"Are you okay?"

I explained the problem: restless kids, absent buses, Dave's resulting game, and that then he said, "Mr. Hamilton says, yell 'Mrs. Wilson is beautiful.'"

Rachel stopped mid-sip and stared at me, eyes wide.

"What?"

"I know, right?" I paced the room. "What's that about?"

"What did you do?" Rachel placed her soda on her desk.

"What could I do? I played along."

"Are you going to talk with him?"

"And say what? 'By the way, Dave, you called me beautiful in front of a bunch of kids.' I am not going there."

"How do you feel?"

Truth was, I wasn't sure. I knew I felt shocked, but at the same time I felt flattered.

Beautiful? Such an intimate word.

"I don't know. I mean it was probably a totally innocent comment, like I'm a beautiful person or a beautiful teacher. On the other hand, it could mean something skeevy, like I'm going to catch him watching me teach through the windows or something." I took a deep breath. "What should I do?"

Rachel shrugged. "What do you want to do?"

I bit my top lip, thinking, and not knowing what I thought.

Over the next few days, I searched Dave's face for some hidden meanings, examined his eyes for suggestive looks, but found nothing.

Still, it had happened. He had said I was beautiful.

I vacillated. Should I tell him how I felt? Should I play it off casually? Should I sit him down for a serious talk about "boundaries"?

In the end, I did nothing.

Except bask in the word "beautiful." I turned the word over in my mind, savoring it like a dark chocolate truffle melting on my tongue.

Maybe I am beautiful, I thought. Maybe you can say someone's beautiful and not have it be creepy and awkward.

Beautiful

As the weeks went by, I felt lighter than I had in a long time, joking and talking with my students.

I found myself searching out and focusing on the qualities that made each one of them beautiful.

As I walked along the hallway to the last bus duty before summer break, I went over the day in my mind. Had I scarred anyone for life? Had I smiled enough?

Was I really meant to teach?

And for once, I knew the answer.

The Midday Gasp

by Sara F. Shacter

MY SANDWICH WAS lucky.

I looked at it sitting there in its plastic bag. Protected.

Here in the faculty cafeteria—no students allowed—I felt protected, too. But fifth-period lunch was going to end, and then I was going to be out there . . . with them.

Erin, or "Miss O'Malley," dropped into her accustomed seat across from me. "Are you going to eat it?"

I slipped my sandwich out of its plastic bag.

Erin and I smiled weakly at each other. We were new hires, both teaching high school English, and we shared an unspoken emotional state, something closer to desperation than hope.

I contemplated my lucky sandwich. Sure, it was getting eaten, but it wasn't getting eaten alive by a bunch of high school students.

Neither my ham, nor my cheese, cared that Shannon, from fourth-period American Literature, liked to smile snarkily and call me "Sara" instead of "Miss Freed."

The mayo shrugged at the fact that I had ninety freshman research papers, collected a week ago, which I hadn't even begun to grade.

The rye bread was absent when I admitted to my seniors that I had made a mistake during our discussion of *Macbeth*. At the time, I had been proud of my decision to fess up. I would not be one of those teachers who couldn't admit errors. But my reward was a shift in the air, rolling eyes, and an unspoken sentence hanging in the air: what an idiot!

Being chewed was one thing. Suffering slings and arrows was something quite different.

A boisterous voice caused me to look around the cafeteria.

A man I recognized from the foreign language department was telling a story, his hands flying through the air as he approached the apex of his tale. When he finally reached the punch line, the entire table broke into laughter.

None of the seasoned teachers seemed aware of the clock as the seconds of lunch ticked by. I just knew, when the bell rang, they would all stroll back to class as if they were on a tropical beach.

I, on the other hand, sat stiff with tension. I watched the clock, bemoaning each minute as it evaporated, bringing me closer to my next class. I never strolled. I scurried.

I knew, in my heart of hearts, that I loved teaching. I loved the students. But I felt as if I were crammed into the bottom of my teacher bag, suffocated by stress, expectations, and lack of sleep.

The table of senior staff moved on to new topics. I began to stare, half expecting to see that each had a magic talisman hidden under a shirt collar or embedded into an earring. I longed for the serenity they enjoyed.

I took a nibble of my lucky sandwich.

"So. How's your day?"

Erin and I shared our highlights, including how entire rainforests had been cleared and stacked neatly on our desks.

Then Erin shared a fantasy she often had while driving to school: a car accident. Oh, nothing serious. She wasn't maimed or anything. Just enough bruising or muscle strain to, you know, put her out of commission for a few weeks. Sort of a forced leave of absence.

A little R & R. Simply add a drink with an umbrella.

Bliss.

I took another bite of ham and cheese.

Talk turned to lesson plans. The usual. I had raced through the material too quickly, resulting in too much time left over. Erin was still deciding what to do with her students during eighth period.

And then she described an activity she had tried with her sophomores.

It involved role-playing. Erin divided her students into groups. Each group drew a slip of paper from a hat. Each slip had the name of a character from the novel they were currently reading. Erin then gave each group a series of questions to help them envision the world from that character's point of view.

I took two hearty bites of sandwich.

Huh. That sounded neat. I could do that with my freshmen. We were studying *Romeo and Juliet*. What if I put Angela, Derek, Brett, and Maggie in a group and told them to pretend they were Juliet? Romeo and Juliet and Juliet and Juliet and Juliet.

Where could I go with that?

I started smiling at the prospect. Brett would crack us up. He'd be Juliet, all right, with a high-pitched Elizabethan accent and perhaps some lovely accessories to boot. But I bet he'd make some insightful points.

I scarfed my apple and chips so I wouldn't have to talk with my mouth full. "Tell me more."

Erin and I started to brainstorm. Her idea lent itself to endless possibilities.

I could bring in some games, and the students could decide which game Juliet would like most and why! Angela and Derek would go to town, arguing about whether Juliet's penchant for speeches made her a Scrabble gal, or whether her melodramatics would make her perfect for charades.

There were countless decisions quadruple—Juliet could make:

Pepperoni or cheese? Why?

Vanilla or chocolate? Why?

Read a challenging Elizabethan play or just rent the movie?

Maybe I could introduce some hypothetical scenarios about cliques and peer pressure. That would certainly fit the text. I bet applying those concepts would open the floodgates for Maggie.

The bell rang. I hadn't even noticed the final minutes tick by.

I popped the last morsel of ham and cheese into my mouth, bid Erin a hasty farewell, and hurried off to class.

Slowed it down to a stroll.

Maybe my sandwich wasn't the lucky one after all.

Special Words

by Clyde L. Borg

"GOOD AFTERNOON, MR. Borg."

After an arduous day at school, I would wearily shuffle to the bus stop to catch my ride home. I was usually a bit down, worrying about my performance that day, and rehashing the things that went wrong.

Being a first-year high school teacher, a lot could go wrong.

On my way to the bus stop, I always seemed to meet up with one of my students, Angelo Arrechi. His name rolled off my tongue.

The diminutive Angelo would greet me with a simple salutation: "Good afternoon, Mr. Borg."

"Good afternoon, Angelo."

"Good afternoon, Mr. Borg." Angelo's words always straightened my spine, reminding me I was a teacher, a position that commanded respect. Those words inspired me to continue and what I was doing, and what I continued to do for the next thirty-seven years.

And then there was Maria.

At the end of the school year, I asked my first-year classes to write course evaluations, a tradition that I have since kept.

I thought I could use the evaluations to improve my teaching ability over the summer, or at least to identify where I most needed improvement.

Maria wrote something very interesting and significant.

She thanked me, not for having taught her well, or for her having learned the subject well, but for having made her smile. "You made me smile."

Maria smiled because of me, and that fact was so important to her that she felt compelled to tell me on the course evaluation.

Her words made me realize that introducing students to the subject matter was not the only effect I had in the classroom. I conveyed more than the dry stuff of academic knowledge. I taught them how to treat education, how to treat other people, and how to treat life, all by example.

While I don't know what I did exactly to make Maria smile, I certainly knew it wasn't because of the course content. It must have been something I did naturally, without thought. Apparently, I had to power to influence my students in many ways outside the bounds of syllabus points.

If I could make them smile, I could also make them sad. If I could make them feel proud, I could also make them feel ashamed. If I could make them excited about their future, I could also make them despair.

I could do any of those things—good and bad—without being aware of my impact at the time. I might never know what effect I'd had if the students didn't speak to me in person or through those course evaluations.

While it only made sense that the students observed and absorbed my every action, I'd never thought of it exactly that way. You wanted the students to focus on you because that meant they were listening.

Maria's comment made me realize that even if the students weren't listening, or even if they listened but didn't understand, they were still learning lessons from my performance.

If I frowned when I heard an administrative announcement, what message was I sending to the students? Disrespect for authority? Impatience? Anger?

If I glanced away while a student was talking to me, what message was I sending the student? Certainly nothing positive.

I was a role model and my influence was enormous. I needed to be knowledgeable, fair, concerned, respectful, and helpful. I needed to think before I reacted to anything, and modify my reactions accordingly.

As a high school teacher, I had a tremendous responsibility to my students, far beyond the scope of curriculum.

"You made me smile."

Maria helped me realize the breadth of my impact.

When I later became an administrator, I knew that I would need to set examples not only for the students, but also for the faculty and staff.

I was vice-principal with my eye on the principal position. When that plan was thwarted, I sank into a depression.

Should I quit my present position? Switch to another school and try to advance there? Chuck my plan and go back to teaching?

What were the faculty and staff saying about my attempt at advancement? Were they secretly glad I'd failed?

Once again, a student came to my rescue. In the school hallway, Christian cast his eyes on me. "Don't worry, Mr. Borg. You're the man."

Once again, simple words lifted my spirits at a difficult time.

While teachers do convey information through attitude and behavior, we primarily rely on words. Some of them are rote. Some of them are special.

None of them are as special as the ones uttered by our students.

Angelo's words boosted my confidence in my first year of teaching. Maria's words helped me become a better teacher. Christian's words supported me in my hour of darkness.

"Good afternoon, Mr. Borg."

"You made me smile."

"Don't worry, Mr. Borg. You're the man."

Simple words but special words, special words from special people whom I will never forget.

The Perfect Mistake

by Andrew McAleer

I KNEW ONE thing for certain that first year I taught at Boston College. Everything would go perfectly. There was no question about it. After all, I had prepared for every contingency.

My syllabus? Check. Submitted a month early. Required reading materials on the campus bookstore shelf? Check. Having heard horror stories about texts never arriving in time for the beginning of a semester, I wasn't taking any chances. I took an afternoon off from work and discovered that the books were in fact shelved and ready for educating.

A dreadful thought occurred to me: Were there enough? After all, I assured myself, my students were going to love me and think I was the best teacher to come along since Mr. Chips. They would tell all their friends to take my course. It was going to be standing room only. Perhaps I would need a lecture hall.

I dashed over to the registrar to take a gander at the class roster. Not bad. Twenty-one students. Utilizing some of my old Dale Carnegie skills I memorized my students' names and majors. By the end of the first week, that number was sure to double.

Class lectures? Check. All outlined, organized by date, and ready to impart knowledge into the pliant minds of my eager students. The only thing left to do now was to get through the first night of class.

Call it stage fright, but my first evening was anything but perfect. Before class Dean Woods had a social gathering for the professors, and afterward an orientation was scheduled. I was teaching a course entitled "The Master Sleuths" and wanted to present him with an inscribed copy of my new mystery novel. I decided to mention the course title in my inscription, and when I did, I became so nervous that I misspelled the word "sleuth," placing the "u" before the "e." Here I was, teaching a crime fiction course and not only did I misspell the title of the course, but I was providing the dean with all the evidence he needed to show me the door.

After the social, it was off to orientation. I looked at my watch. It was 6:15 P.M. Class began at 6:30. How could orientation possibly last a mere quarter hour? The dean must be losing it. At 6:27 I shot out of my chair and, in front of hundreds of spectators, hot-footed it out of the auditorium. All these other fools could be late for class, but not I.

No time to wait for the elevator, so I double-timed it up three flights of stairs and ran into the classroom expecting a grand reception Holmes himself might have envied. No one was there. Not even a custodian closing up the joint.

I began to panic. Maybe everyone dropped my class? Did I assign too many books? Six wasn't too many, was it? I better check with the dean's office. His cheerful secretary allayed my fears about mass withdrawal and reminded me that on orientation night, class begins at 7:30 P.M.

Okay, so I had a couple of blunders under my belt before class even began, but that was okay, my lecture was sure to be a smash hit. I was a believer in the Socratic method of teaching and planned on offering a few topics that would undoubtedly end in lively debate.

There was just one problem with my strategy—I was the one who was supposed to be teaching them the topics to debate. Who was the better hard-boiled author, Raymond Chandler or Dashiell Hammett? Are suspense novels simply mystery novels wrapped up in a new package? Does the modern thriller contain too much romance? Is Edgar Allan Poe really the father of the modern detective story?

How would my students know when I hadn't gone over the subject matter with them yet?

Let's just say I'm lucky orientation shaved an hour off class that evening.

One of my favorite Celtics players was M. L. Carr, who was part of the Celtics dynasty in the 1980s. He was not the best player on the team, but he could never just sit on the bench and watch the game slip by. No matter how bad things looked, he was always up waving a towel, running up and down the court, and cheering his teammates. He made them and the spectators believe. I got as much excitement out of watching him as I did watching Larry Bird sink three-pointers at the buzzer.

Maybe I'm a little like M. L. Carr: I'm not the best teacher, not by a longshot, but I love teaching. I get to teach healthy things to people that they previously did not know. And somehow, when that classroom empties for the night, it is me who walks away learning something new. Don't ever forget that: Learn from your students.

The Perfect Mistake

Prepare as best you can for your first year of teaching—and your last! But don't expect to be perfect; you'll only let yourself down. As my fifth-grade math teacher Miss Wall used to remind me, "We all make mistakes. That's why God put erasers at the end of pencils."

It may sound cliché, but we do learn from our mistakes. They make us more compassionate. They help us appreciate the student who is really trying, but still having a difficult time on what we may consider an easy point. Mistakes make us human. Students appreciate that.

When I Breathed I Clinked

by Michael Keyton

How I DRIFTED INTO teaching, how I stuck with it for thirty years, still remains a bit of a mystery. Perhaps I just liked teaching history—working with young and irreverent minds, and the feeling that there wasn't anything else I really wanted to do.

Marking a class roster for the first time was an exercise in poetry. Names like "Giovanni Ambroselli" and "Rudolpho Velluchi" rolled off the tongue like incantations, putting me in a good mood for the rest of the day. The boys were almost as magical as their names, and it was hard to discipline them with a straight face, looking into eyes that whirled me back to my childhood in a rough Liverpool school.

It was an act of opportunism. Two boys, finishing a morning paper route, kept their large canvas bags, perhaps in readiness for the evening delivery that followed school; perhaps not. En route to the school, they walked into a sweet-shop and watched as the shopkeeper stepped into the back for a fresh box of gum. A moment later, four very large jars of pear drops and mints disappeared into the two canvas bags, and the boys walked out, backs unnaturally stiff beneath twelve pounds of sweets.

They didn't have far to go. The school was just down the road. Nor did the shopkeeper need very long to work out what had happened. The Headmaster received the phone call within the hour.

A special assembly for the whole school.

Unprecedented.

No one knew for sure whether the whole school would fit in the hall.

We were lined up by grades, the teachers leaning against walls, arms folded, and with knowing prison-guard smiles on their faces. The Headmaster paced the stage like an aging lion.

The lion delivered his bombshell. A shopkeeper was accusing two of our boys of theft. Four empty sweet jars had been found in the toilets. We were to stand in silence while staff searched our pockets. Teachers swung away from the walls, some of them grim, others with menacing smiles.

Sweets cascaded from every pocket.

"I am Spartacus," mumbled eight hundred sugar-encrusted lips. The film was still four years away.

The Headmaster played his final card, albeit a very weak one. He called in the shopkeeper, who'd apparently been standing hidden behind the stage curtains. The shopkeeper looked nervous, like someone who'd rather be anywhere else. The poor man stared into our faces one by one as the Headmaster thundered in frustration from the stage.

Finally it was over, and we stood there in silence, all of the students missing their break as a form of collective punishment.

My First Year in the Classroom

What goes around comes around. Now I was one of those teachers—different school, different boys—but about to experience something remarkably similar.

St. Johns was my first teaching job, and I'd been given the wildest class in the school. "To break you in," an elderly teacher told me in a mournful voice.

It was Christmas, the last day of term. The weather was wintry, the schoolyard crusted in a thin skin of snow.

I was on break duty, looking forward to the holiday starting in two hours, twenty-one minutes, and ten seconds' time. A member of my class came up to me. "Merry Christmas, sir," he said. He thrust a small bottle of whiskey at me.

My spirits rose. Just two hours, eighteen minutes and twenty-one seconds to go—and a bottle of whiskey!

In the next ten minutes my spirits rose still further as one by one the boys in my class came up to me, each offering me various alcoholic drinks, each wishing me a Merry Christmas. Teaching wasn't so bad, I decided. I could come to like this.

The bell went and we trooped into the final assembly of the year. The hall was freezing, the central heating having been switched off in readiness for the holiday ahead. I stood there in my woolen greatcoat, its many pockets bulging with bottles.

When I breathed, I clinked.

My class was positioned as usual in the front row, staring up at the stage with their usual intentness. In my first week, I'd assumed they were just keen, inspired perhaps by the Headmaster's various homilies.

In my second week, as I came to know the Headmaster and my class, I realized this couldn't be so.

In my third week, I discovered the truth. My class had a sweepstakes on how many times the Headmaster rocked on his feet as he spoke. Real money changed hands.

But the Headmaster had something serious to say today. Boys had brought alcohol into the school. A boy had been caught sick in the caretaker's cupboard. Everyone—he stared at my class in particular—would be searched.

The staff swung away from the walls with the same menacing smiles I remembered from all those years ago. I walked carefully, aware of every tiny clink.

My class stood up, impassive, obedient, their gaze fixed intently on the Headmaster's shoes.

I patted them down, avoiding their eyes, aware of the smirking behind them. No matter, just over an hour to go.

No drink was found, and I returned to the wall, contemplating an unexpectedly rich and exciting Christmas. The Lord works in mysterious ways. As I walked to the bus stop there was movement behind me. I turned.

"Can we have our bottles back, sir?"

The optimism of youth.

"Merry Christmas, boys," I said.

And I meant it.

Learning to Say Goodbye

by K. L. James

I WAS JUST finishing up my first year teaching high school biology in an inner city school in the Midwest. The students were challenging, but I felt I was making progress, making a difference in their lives. They might not go on to become biologists, but they had learned.

On the Saturday night before my last week of school, I was watching television when my phone rang unexpectedly.

I said, "Hello," and after a short pause I heard the monotone voice of my principal on the other end.

"Hello, Kelly, this is Mr. Haynes. I just wanted to call and let you know that one of your students, Marco, is dead. He was found in a park with a bag over his head. The police think he committed suicide. I'll let you know more details when I get them. Goodbye."

The call ended as abruptly as it had started.

I slowly dropped onto my couch and stared into space. It could not be true. Marco had been one of my favorite students, and I thought he had a bright future. How could he have killed himself? Why? It just didn't make any sense.

As I sat alone in my house, I could see his smiling face and hear him telling me about the latest book he was reading. Marco loved to read.

Tears started to burn in my eyes as guilt washed over me.

How many times had I only half-listened to what Marco was saying? How many times had I pushed him aside to help students I thought were more needy? If only I had taken the time to listen, had responded differently, would Marco still be alive?

I spent the rest of the night crying and questioning everything I had done as a teacher.

On Monday morning, I reluctantly got dressed and headed for school.

The first five periods went by in a blur. There was sadness, disbelief, and anger, but I knew that the reactions would pale in comparison to those felt by the students who had been with Marco in my sixth-period class.

Although most of Marco's class had been seniors who were already out of school, I still had eight juniors left. I had no idea how they would react to the death of their classmate, and I knew I was not prepared to help them cope with their loss.

I was having a hard enough time with my own feelings.

When sixth period began, I walked up to the front of the room. One of my students raised her hand, her tears representing how I felt.

"Can I move? Marco used to sit beside me."

"Of course."

I talked to my class for a few more minutes about Marco, and then I turned on a Star Wars movie. Marco had loved science fiction, and watching the movie together seemed a suitable tribute to his memory.

We sat in a small circle and cried while the movie played in the background. Somehow, we made it through that class period. When the bell rang I said goodbye and wiped away my tears.

Then I greeted my next class with a small smile.

When the last bell of the day finally rang, I packed up my belongings and left.

Instead of going to my house, I went to the funeral home. The family wanted a closed funeral, but they were allowing visitation that afternoon.

I walked into the funeral parlor and signed the book. The entire room was completely silent as I walked up to the front of the room to say goodbye. Marco was dressed in his blue graduation robes with a nice suit underneath. His face was solemn and he was no longer smiling.

It was hard to believe that someone so full of life was now completely still and empty. As tears threatened to spill, I looked away from his coffin. That was when I saw his diploma sitting on a nearby stool and I instantly broke into tears.

I stayed in the room for several more minutes until I had to say goodbye. As I left, I passed his mother and mumbled a brief "I'm sorry."

I walked back to my car fighting back tears. As I drove away, I decided to go to a nearby grocery store, where I bought a box of chocolate chip cookies and a pint of ice cream.

When I got home, I gorged on the junk food, and then got dressed for graduation. I tried to put on a smile before I left. I wanted to do my best to help my seniors enjoy their night.

When I got there, I was amazed how happy the students were. Their happiness was infectious, and before long I found myself laughing and smiling with them. Although I had lost one student, I realized my hard work had made a difference in the lives of many others.

That night, I went home emotionally and physically exhausted.

Part of me wanted to find a new career. Teaching was tougher than anybody ever told me. It was so much more than standing in front of a room and giving out assignments. It included becoming an integral part of the lives of students and their families, and with that came a huge responsibility.

Was I still up for that challenge?

Yes, I decided. I knew I would never push another student to the side again. I knew that, as a teacher, my most important job was serving my students and preparing them for their future.

Over the years, I have seen many students that remind me of Marco.

I always take the time to listen.

Left

by Emily Warren

I LEFT MY heart on 135th and Lenox.

I walked away in wobbly heels and run-down stockings, down toward the 2 train. Spring taunted the rush hour of post-dismissal teenagers, holding hands over their eyes to block the sun hanging from a reborn, metallic sky.

I cast my students a quick glance, and was gone.

I left the piles of kids, with high yells that push an adult's headache closer to its brink. I left the laughter that makes others jealous or hateful or both. I left them standing like an almost-boiling pot of water, in worn uniforms or long white T-shirts, black or red bandanas hanging from back pockets, bubbly behinds bunched beneath black and silver belts. I left their freedom, surfacing in pounding palms, or "Sup Yo!" greetings, or head-shaking smiles.

I left the hour of freedom my students held so dearly, that hour between school and home. I walked past as they offered to share it with me, flashing welcome from the light palms of their dark hands. It was fleeting; it would pass.

I left my heart up there with that freedom, half-inch heels clacking down the steps. This descent once took focus. Now, it had become natural, like bare feet in some summer way-back-when whose soles have gotten used to the slippery contours of algae-covered rocks.

Clack by clack, grip by grip, down into the warmer, wetter 135th Street station, I left the island of my Harlem behind.

Sounds grew distant: prices of winter hats in May, the barefoot man with white calloused toes asking for a cigarette, a quarter. Traffic and horns and shouts of outrage.

My bag was heavy, its straps digging into soft shoulder skin, holding my companions for the train ride home: souvenirs. Their quizzes, their letters, their papers titled "A Rats View of 117th" or "My Block."

Down into the dungeon of the 135th Street station, I nodded "what up" to the second metro lane, out of order since January.

Even with a trail of dried black mascara leading down the pale skin beneath my eyes, this could have been any other day.

Rewind, delete, reword:

It was a day, like any other.

Only when I searched for boundaries that weaseled their way in between "then" and "now" did I feel a difference.

My hair was knotted, my back salty from dried sweat, my fingers covered with marker from an overhead projector.

It was a day, like any other.

The difference: I'd never be their teacher again.

I realized this after I sat on the cold blue subway seats, my bag rested on sweaty knees. I'd never be their teacher again.

My First Year in the Classroom

It wasn't until the train fell toward the downtown of "can you make that soy with no-whip?" and Jeep-like baby strollers with white babies rolled by brown ladies that I realized what I'd left behind, on those funny curious uptown streets of Harlem.

My heart. I'd left my heart on 135th and Lenox.

Have you ever left something behind that should be with you? A wallet, a favorite book, an untouched turkey sandwich, an umbrella in the rain? I've put my heart through hell and back, caused it to pound and slow and shatter. I'd treated it badly and allowed others to do the same.

But never, ever, had I left it behind.

Only my first year teaching and already this heart had been intimidated, antagonized, accepted, loved, forgiven, idolized, ignored, named "Whitey" and "Miss Warren G" or "Miss G" for short.

This heart had been misunderstood, believed in, begged to dance the White-Lady Dance, robbed, humiliated, whole-heartedly thanked, and let go.

Now, apparently, the hourglass had run dry and it was time to move on. Simple as that.

Moving . . . fine. But moving on?

This motion just didn't seem linear, a natural progression. I didn't want to trade the seventy-five-cent Tropicana juices grabbed from the bodega and chugged in the faculty room for the world of chilled martini glasses with ice cubes and soda water.

I didn't want to trade a world painfully real for a game of flirt and frolic.

How would I escape the escape?

Left

Leaving my teacher-life behind for the summer felt like the opposite of evolution—a devolution if you will—like amputating a leg after winning a marathon, or burning down a newly purchased home.

I sent myself back, back past the benches covered with graffiti, back through the haze of Kennedy's fried chicken and beef patties, back the long way to Lenox Avenue.

There was my heart, being where it was at.

Soaking that world like a sponge.

The smells. The sights. The sounds.

The throbbing life.

It was a day, like any other.

And then I let it go.

Closing

Dear readers, I want to thank you for being such good listeners.
Class dismissed.

Stephen D. Rogers

Contributor Biographies

Nancy Kelly Allen has been a social worker, elementary school teacher, and librarian. As an award-winning writer, she has produced seven picture books and one chapter book, as well as her writing for adults.

Michelle Blackley operates her own literary publicity firm, Don't Judge a Book by its Cover, in Buffalo, New York. She is also an adjunct lecturer of communication at Buffalo State College and volunteers her publicity talents for Project F.L.I.G.H.T., a literary program for families.

Sharon Blumberg is a freelance writer and junior high Spanish teacher. She is also a staff member of the National Writing for Children's Center, and works on the board of the Story Circle Network, an organization that encourages women to tell their unique life stories.

Clyde L. Borg served as a high school social studies and English teacher for thirty-eight years. Retired, he works part-time in adult education and as a mentor to new secondary teachers. Some of his work has appeared in *Cause & Effect* magazine, *The Verse Marauder*, *Fate* magazine, *Capper's*, *Nostalgia* magazine, and *Skipping Stones* magazine.

Barri L. Bumgarner spent a decade in a junior high classroom. Her first YA novel, *Dregs*, tackles the tough issues of bullies, steroids, and what it takes to push a teenager to bring a gun to school. It won the Walter Williams Major Work Award, runner-up, 2007. Learn more at *www .barriLbumgarner.com*.

Albert W. Caron, Jr., is a veteran Massachusetts middle school English teacher who has been nominated to Who's Who Among America's Teachers five times. He is a member of the Lincoln Group of Boston, the Civil War Round Table of New Bedford, and the Marion Writers Group.

Ed Dwyer taught in grades four, six, and seven and worked as a reading clinician for five years. He currently teaches at East Tennessee State University in Johnson City, where he is in the Department of Curriculum and Instruction. He works with students who wish to teach in an elementary school.

Terri Elders, LCSW, has seen her stories appear in over a dozen anthologies, including such series as *A Cup of Comfort*, *Chicken Soup for the Soul*, and *Literary Cottage Hero*. In 2006 she received the UCLA Alumni Association Community Service Award for her work with both Peace Corps and AmeriCorps VISTA. Write to her at *telders@hotmail.com*.

Dr. Bobby R. Ezell taught English for many years at the junior high, high school, and college levels. He now teaches in the Department of Curriculum and Instruction at Sam Houston State University in Huntsville, Texas, working with future teachers in the teacher education program.

Dr. Andrea S. Foster is an assistant professor of science education at Sam Houston State University in Hunstville, Texas. She has been the recipient of numerous teaching honors including the Presidential Award for Excellence in Science Teaching and the 2008 College of Education Teaching Excellence Award.

Marie Dixon Frisch is a therapeutic clown, writer, and English teacher by day in Hamburg, Germany. She has written a clown series for the former UK magazine *oneUp*, and been published in *Alternatives Journal*, *Woman's Own*, *Guide*, *My Weekly*, *Best*, and others.

Rachel Garlinghouse is a composition lecturer at Southern Illinois University–Edwardsville. When Rachel is not teaching, she is freelance writing for various publications including those that focus on health and adoption.

Tina Haapala began substitute teaching to help out her community and to determine whether teaching would be the career change she was looking for. Some of her recent work has appeared in the *Chicken Soup for the Soul* books, *Teens Talk Middle School* and *Getting in . . . to College*. She can be contacted at *tinahaapala@gmail.com*.

Mindy Hardwick is a published children's writer and educator. She teaches courses for educators at Seattle Pacific University and runs a weekly poetry workshop with teens at Denney Juvenile Justice Center. Mindy began her career by teaching seventh-grade language arts in Lake Stevens, Washington. You can find out more about Mindy at *www.mindyhardwick.com*.

Melinda Huynh is currently teaching first grade within the Westminster School District, CA. After so many of her own teachers impacted her life, she decided to go into teaching so that she could positively influence as many other people as possible. She enjoys family time, surfing, reading, and Tahitian dancing.

K. L. James studied biology at the University of Nebraska at Lincoln and then received her master's degree in secondary teaching. She started her career at a nearby inner-city school, and is now married to a teacher. They have two children.

Gail Carter Johnson thought her first year as librarian would be her worst year, but found in looking back that it was one of her fondest memories. She became friends with Mrs. Crawford and retired as Dean of

Learning Resources at a community college in North Carolina, where she now writes.

Michael Keyton has cooked in hospital kitchens, taught history in a challenging state school, and played for a number of years in a ceilidh band. His published short stories include "Martin Brownlow's Cat" in *Twisted Cat Tales*, "Bony Park" in *To Be Read by Dawn Vol. III*, and "Beside the Seaside" in *Strange Stories of Sand and Sea*.

Teresa Ives Lilly received her degree in education, special education, and was certified as a reading specialist. She is the editor of the online children's magazine *www.Kidzwonder.com* as well as the creator of more than 100 unit studies, which can be found at *www.hshighlights.com*.

Beverly C. Lucey is a freelance writer. She has an essay titled "Are We Teaching Yet?" in *A Cup of Comfort® for Teachers*, and stories within several other anthologies.

Dr. Sharon A. Lynch is chair of the Department of Language, Literacy and Special Populations at Sam Houston State University. Her primary interests lie in the areas of assessment and learners with significant educational needs.

Andrew McAleer is an adjunct professor at Boston College and the author of five books, including the #1 bestselling *Mystery Writing in a Nutshell* and *The 101 Habits of Highly Successful Novelists*. He works as a prosecutor with the Massachusetts Department of Correction. Visit him at *www.crimestalkers.com*.

Kathleen A. Montgomery was hired at Bennet-Hemenway School in Natick, Massachusetts, while she was still a senior at Boston University. With the exception of two years of teaching third grade, she has spent the majority of her career teaching second. She earned her master's degree, master's plus 30, and master's plus 60.

Beth Morrissey holds an MLIS from the National University of Ireland and began her career as an international school librarian in Dublin city. She now works as a full-time freelance writer and teaches adults about writing through the University College Dublin Adult Education Centre. Visit Beth at *www.bethmorrissey.com*.

Judy Nickles spent two years as a short-term missionary in the Democratic Republic of the Congo (then Zaire) teaching at the American School of Kinshasa. After marrying the Presbyterian mission pilot, she spent two years at his station in Kananga before returning to the United States, where she taught in private and public schools.

Linda O'Connell has been an early childhood educator in St. Louis, Missouri, for more than thirty years. Students leave their handprints all over Ms. Linda's classroom and on her heart. She is also a multigenre writer; her prose, poetry, and early education articles appear in numerous publications.

Yuria R. Orihuela came to the United States from Cuba at the age of fourteen. She taught twenty-one years in the Miami-Dade Public Schools before becoming a district mathematics supervisor and then taught at Miami Dade College for two years. She is the author of several mathematics textbooks.

Diane Payne teaches creative writing at University of Arkansas–Monticello. She is the author of two novels, *Burning Tulips* and *A New Kind of Music*, and has been published in hundreds of literary magazines. More info can be found at *http://home.earthlink.net/~dianepayne*.

Susan Peters served as a Peace Corps volunteer in Poland, and continued teaching in Russia, China, Japan, Iceland, and Mexico (where she finally learned some Spanish). She then spent four years teaching at a college in

Germany before returning to her Kansas roots. Currently, she is an adjunct assistant professor at Johnson County Community College.

Nancy Polny has been fortunate to work with children in many ways: room parent, Confraternity of Christian Doctrine (CCD) teacher, Religious Education Coordinator, nanny, and classroom teacher. She's taught kindergarten, first grade, and second grade in both public and private schools.

Jessica Polny likes art, science, drama, reading, and writing in her free time. Looking to see what her mother was doing on the computer, she couldn't stop herself from editing her mother's story.

Felice Prager is a freelance writer from Scottsdale, Arizona, with credits in local, national, and international publications. In addition to writing, she also works with adults and children who have moderate to severe learning disabilities as a multisensory educational therapist. Please visit her blog, Felice Prager Writes Funny!, at *www.writefunny.blogspot.com*.

T. Lloyd Reilly has been a truck driver, equipment operator, ranch manager, HIV/AIDS counselor, market researcher, short-order cook, bouncer, taxi driver, soldier, explosives handler, telemarketer, suicide counselor, halfway house manager, rock 'n' roll roadie, dispatcher, industrial safety consultant, literacy instructor, industrial trainer, roughneck, construction worker, and, most important of all, an English teacher.

Kimberlee Rizzitano lives in Massachusetts, where she is a fourth-grade teacher at St. Tarcisius Elementary School. In her spare time she loves to write children's stories, and frequently shares her picture books with her class. She enjoys gardening, playing with her kids, computer games, and traveling.

Stephen D. Rogers has taught at the middle school, high school, and college level. He has also taught continuing education and online courses to adults, as well as the workshops offered by the nonprofit organization Literature Is For Everybody, Inc. His stories have appeared in *My Teacher Is My Hero*.

Dorit Sasson successfully taught English language learners in various schools in Israel for eleven years before returning to the United States in the summer of 2007. She is the creator of the New Teacher Resource Center: *www.newteacherresourcecenter.com*.

Beth Schart has a master's degree in elementary education and has been teaching for almost twenty years in Coventry, Rhode Island. She has completed a middle grade novel and has several more in the works. She is married with three grown children.

Jacqueline Seewald has taught English at the middle school and high school levels as well as technical, expository, and creative writing at the college level. She has also worked as an academic librarian and educational media specialist.

Sara F. Shacter taught high school English for ten wonderful years. Her fiction debut, the picture book *Heading to the Wedding*, is available from Red Rock Press. Sara loves visiting schools and talking to students about writing. Please visit her at *www.sarafshacter.com*.

Susanne Shaphren's nonfiction and fiction for readers of all ages has appeared in an eclectic alphabet soup of online and print venues including *Absolute Write*, *Children's Digest*, *Children's Playmate*, *Espresso Fiction*, *Golden Years*, *Jack and Jill*, *Mystery Writers of America Presents Show Business Is Murder*, *The Irascible Professor*, and *The Writer*.

Camille Subramaniam lives with her husband, Sudhagar, and son, Xavier, in St. Charles, Missouri. She writes by day and teaches writing by night at Southern Illinois University–Edwardsville. Camille enjoys spending time with her family, who live very close, and her husband's family, who live in faraway Malaysia. Luckily, she also enjoys travel and adventure.

Rosemary Troxel graduated from ISU in Normal, Illinois, and began her teaching career at Kimes Elementary School in Streator, where she taught fourth grade. Over the next twenty-plus years, she taught grades one and three through eight as well as community college students.

Robin Amada Tzucker graduated from the University of California, Santa Cruz, in 1985 and began teaching that same year in Richmond, California. After staying home with her children, she returned to her first love, working as a classroom teacher in an elementary school.

Emily Warren lives, teaches, waitresses, and bartends in New York City. Her parents blessed her with the opportunity to receive one strand of topnotch education, and her students have blessed her with another extraordinary strand. Her dream is to somehow live a life that repays them both.

Monica Whitaker teaches a class of immigrant and refugee students in Nashville, Tennessee. Whitaker, a former journalist, chronicles her pedagogical adventures in a tattered, much-loved journal. Outside the classroom, she studies and instructs at her husband's martial arts school, and she enjoys taking long hikes in the woods.

Billie Wilson graduated from Winthrop College in 1954 and taught at Wampee–Little River High for a year before traipsing after her new, knowledge-seeking spouse from South Carolina to Virginia, to Maryland, and finally to Georgia, teaching English at each stop. She's published stories in *O Georgia* anthologies, in *Athens* magazine, and *Southern Distinction*.

Contributor Biographies

Kelly Wilson is a busy mother, teacher, and writer. Kelly has been creating characters and stories since she was in elementary school. She has been teaching for nine years, and currently lives with her husband and children in Gladstone, Oregon. You can read more about her at *www.wilsonwrites.com*.

Kari-Lynn Winters is an award-winning children's author (*www.kariwinters.com*) and performer (*www.tickletrunkplayers.com*) who enjoys being in the classroom in any capacity. She taught in North Carolina for three years and in Toronto for two. She holds a teaching degree from the University of Toronto in regular and special education for children (ages one through thirteen).